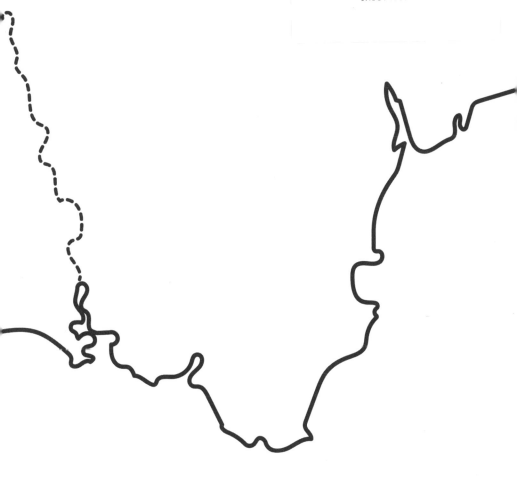

Discover Cornwall

www.maverickguide.co.uk

@maverick.guide

EDITOR & DESIGN

Gabriella Dyson

OUR TALENTED TEAM

Editorial Assistant & Feature Writer: Rachael Brown

Feature Writers: Lucy Studley, Sophie Farrah

Sub Editors: Amy Kilburn, Molly Dyson

Cover Photo: Wheal Coates by George Cryer Photography

Editor's Photo: Tessa Bricknell

Special Thanks: Tom Litten, Chris & Collette Dyson, Barney the Cat

GET IN TOUCH

Editorial: editor@maverickguide.co.uk

Work with us: partnerships@maverickguide.co.uk

INSTAGRAM

@maverick.guide

MAVERICKGUIDE.CO.UK

A Maverick

/mav(ə)rik/ | NOUN

A person who thinks and acts
independently, often behaving
differently from the expected
or usual way.

"Dynnargh dhywgh"

In 2020, we published our very first Cornwall travel guide. At the time, we were working on a shoestring budget with a tiny freelance team and the small factor of a national lockdown prohibiting travel.
So, you can imagine our surprise when our little guidebook started flying off the shelves! It seems that many of you share our enthusiasm for this fabulous county and are ready to embrace Kernow's hidden gems and indie businesses. So, it is my absolute pleasure to present you with volume two of the guide. Over the next 200 pages, we share more of our recommendations for things to see and do in Cornwall, as well as a few insider tips to make your next visit a special one. Enjoy!

Gabriella Dyson

Editor & Founder

EXPLORE CORNWALL

DISCOVER MORE

Coombeshead Farm, Photos by Artur Trixllski, Oscar Holgado

Coombeshead Farm

Lewannick

Roaming the lush Cornish countryside by the Devon border are the flocks of sheep, herds of pigs and a dedicated group of people that make up Coombeshead Farm: a guesthouse and working farm set amongst 66 acres of meadow and oak-lined stream. The restaurant at Coombeshead Farm has all the homely warmth of a farmhouse kitchen, and like a welcome lodger, you can relax at one of their thick oak tables, waiting to be treated to all their current produce and offerings. With a focus on sustainably produced food, expect to eat seasonal ingredients from the surrounding fields as well as pickled, fermented and foraged treats. For the ultimate indulgence, you could sleepover in their converted farmhouse or grain store, both decked out in cosy luxury, with calming neutral hues, walk-in showers and super king beds for a restful night's sleep.

Maverick tip: Coombeshead has recently opened a farm shop allowing guests to stock up on pickles, cordials, meat, dairy and all the produce of their harvest.

coombesheadfarm.co.uk

Rose Cottage

port isaac

For a dreamy stay cosying up by the sea, book the truly one-of-a-kind Rose Cottage. Located on Port Isaac's historic Dolphin Street, just a short stroll from the main harbour, this blushed pink fisherman's cottage has earned quite the reputation for its stylish and characterful interiors.

Lovingly restored by award-winning interior designer, Noushka Design, the cottage sleeps up to six guests in three ocean inspired bedrooms. Downstairs, a bespoke kitchen features white quartz worktops and hand-painted kitchen cabinets, while feature walls and eccentric furnishings bring the living and dining rooms to life.

Maverick tip: If Rose Cottage is fully booked, it's worth checking out its equally beautiful sister-property, Hillside Cottage (see next page).

Book via John Bray Cornish Holidays
www.johnbraycornishholidays.co.uk

Hillside Cottage

port isaac

This family-friendly accommodation is less than a minute's walk down to Port Isaac's vibrant harbour. The ground floor is the main hub of the cottage, where you'll find a stunning handmade kitchen and an open plan living area, decked out by the talented Noushka Design. After a busy day on the coast, it's the perfect space to unwind and watch a movie or play board games by the fire.

Head upstairs to reach the darling master bedroom, with its elegant double bed and views looking of the harbour. Elsewhere, there's a colourful single bedroom and shower room, as well as a dormitory-style bedroom on the top floor with three bespoke-built cabin beds. Guests also have access to a private landscaped rear garden that has been beautifully terraced to provide a practical space for al fresco dining.

Maverick tip: If you pack your walking boots, head west to Port Quin; there's a spectacular walk along the way and the National Trust owned cove is a lovely spot for wild swimming or kayaking.

Book via John Bray Cornish Holidays
www.johnbraycornishholidays.co.uk

discover

Port Isaac

Curated by Rachæl Brown

Your North Cornwall holiday wouldn't be complete without a trip to the beautiful village of Port Isaac. Not only is this diminutive destination extremely quaint, it was also the backdrop to hit television series Doc Martin and is home to the famed musical group Fisherman's Friends. An active fishing village since the early fourteenth century, Port Isaac is best known for its narrow streets, white-washed cottages and traditional granite houses. But there's so much more to discover during your visit...

THE MOTE

The Mote Restaurant sits right on the slipway and if it doesn't lure you in with its perfect location and historic charm, it'll tempt you with its menu of fresh Cornish produce. No doubt you'll be leaving the restaurant satisfied after a hearty plate of food and an evening drink. Word on the grapevine is that the fish pie is so good it's won awards (we know what we're having).

OLD SCHOOL HOUSE

This characterful restaurant and hotel sits atop a green cliff with commanding views of Port Isaac. It serves some delicious food but it's worth checking out for the postcard-worthy scenery alone. Sit and enjoy your meal as you watch the harbour's calm comings and goings. If the weather is fine they also have an outside decking area.

CORNISH ROCK TORS

Jump out of your comfort zone (with the reassurance of a guide) and plunge into the deep with Cornish Rock Tors. These adventure junkies will lead you through adrenaline-fuelled coasteering sessions or take you to nearby hidden bays and sea caves on kayaks or paddle boards.

NATHAN OUTLAW

It wouldn't be Port Isaac without the presence of acclaimed chef Nathan Outlaw. Feast on the absolute best of the Cornish catch at one of his two seafood restaurants in the village. Both restaurants are about as laid-back and cosy as Michelin-star fine dining gets. From Outlaw's New Road, you can sit back and enjoy outstanding food with sensational views of the coast below. Meanwhile, Outlaw's Fish Kitchen sits close to the harbour, so you can watch on as the day's catch is brought in from the sea. A word of warning – parking in Port Isaac can be hard to come by. While there's a carpark next door to Outlaw's New Road, during peak season you may want to hire a taxi or give yourself plenty of time to walk down the hill from the bigger carpark up top.

KILN

If browsing local pottery sounds up your alley, visit Kiln. This design-led studio can be found on one of Port Isaac's many winding streets, right in the heart of the village. Discover their range of unique ceramics, art pieces, Scandinavian homeware and Cornish gifts. Designs are inked and painted by Sue Pullin and all the bone china is fired in kilns in their Port Isaac studio.

PORT QUIN

Just along the North coast from Port Isaac is the quiet cove of Port Quin. It's an idyllic little inlet, popular with walkers and kayakers, that used to be a fishing port. Admire its unspoilt shoreline by following the coastal path. This is a more private spot for those seeking peace and quiet.

DOC MARTIN'S 'PORTWENN'

Of course, a trip to this iconic fishing village wouldn't be complete without discovering some of the destinations made famous by Doc Martin. Port Isaac plays the fictional Cornish village of 'Portwenn' in the television series, which is interestingly enough the old name of nearby Port Quin.

Fern Cottage is arguably one of the most recognisable Doc Martin locations, drawing fans from all over the world to flock to Doctor Ellingham's surgery. You can find the granite-fronted house on the cliffside by walking 100 metres past the harbour and up the hill towards the coast path for Port Quin.

In the village itself you'll recognise The Liberal Club as the village shop in the series, while Doc Martin's local is The Golden Lion pub, which is often filled with the cast and crew during filming. A handful of private residences double as locations for the show, including Mrs Tishell's chemist shop which is a house called Little Dolphins in Middle Street. Central Garage on New Road is the show's fruit and veg shop, while Louisa's home on Fore Street and Bert's Restaurant are only a short stroll from Fern Cottage.

The Golden Lion Pub

Padstow Townhouse

padstow

On a peaceful street in the heart of Padstow you'll find this extraordinary boutique hotel located in an 18th century townhouse. The aptly named Padstow Townhouse offers six uniquely styled suites to choose from and is conveniently located alongside the iconic Paul Ainsworth at No. 6 restaurant. Each suite takes its name from a sweet treat - Bon Bon, Honeycomb, Toffee Apple - and is kitted out with all manner of creature comforts and luxurious furnishings. Pampering comes courtesy of Bloom Remedies, with exclusive 'Serenity Slumber' products created especially for the Townhouse.

Maverick tip: The onsite Kitchen Pantry and honesty bar is kept well stocked with tasty nibbles and evening aperitifs, but if the midnight munchies catch you in the meantime there's always the personal minibar.

paul-ainsworth.co.uk/padstow-townhouse

Molesworth Manor

nr Padstow

Nestled in the attractive hamlet of Little Petherick, just five minutes from Padstow, lies an exquisite 17th century country home with a thoroughly 21st century attitude. Molesworth Manor is one of north Cornwall's most exclusive holiday rentals, offering guests seven en suite luxury bedrooms, its own private wellness spa - with two cedar clad hot tubs and sauna - a spacious cinema room, a dedicated tasting room and gym.

Décor blends together the buildings original heritage with contemporary design, the results of which could be plucked straight from the pages of Architectural Digest. Meanwhile, the manor gardens have been sensitively landscaped with native flora and fauna. There's an almost secret garden ambiance to the grounds, so you're free to discover your own quiet places to relax and unwind.

Maverick tip: The manor concierge service is on hand to provide recommendations for private chefs, massage therapists, fresh crab and lobster, and local surf instructors.

Book via Cornish Gems:
www.cornishgems.com

Newquay

Famed for its great surf and laid-back party culture, the town of Newquay is a popular haunt for surfers and the young at heart. There's more to this town than the waves and the night life though. Here's our pick of the best places to eat, sleep and explore in Cornwall's surf capital:

EXPLORE

Stray away from the town centre and head for the most picturesque part of town: Newquay Harbour. Here you'll find a small, sheltered beach that's a safe spot for wild swimming. The harbour is also overlooked by several cafes and pubs, so you can enjoy the view with a drink in hand.

The iconic Fistral Beach is not to be missed. This natural playground is home to surf schools, restaurants, shops and a calendar of exciting events throughout the year. Fistral Beach Hire Centre has a vast variety of equipment for hire, from paddle boards to longboards. Next door you'll find Fistral Beach Surf School who provide professional coaching for surfers of all levels. The Fistral Fish House is a popular restaurant, where Paul Harwood and family serve a menu of locally caught fish and shellfish. Meanwhile, Fistral Beach Bar gets some of the best sunsets in town from its open aired terrace.

Alternatively, head to Trenance Gardens to soak up the greenery. There's plenty of children's activities and it's a lovely spot to stretch your legs.

FORE STREET CAFE BAR

While this cafe is unassuming from the outside, it serves up some delicious food that has made it a popular local haunt. Expect everything from simple cooked breakfasts to warming soups. There's always a vegan and gluten free option on the menu, as well as delicious hot drinks such as turmeric and vanilla lattes.

BOX & BARBER

This indie coffeehouse (above) is owned and run by brothers Damian and Olly. Perfectly situated between Newquay town centre and Fistral Beach, it's the perfect pre and post-surf stop off. Expect delicious artisan coffees, colourful açai bowls, and all manner of tasty brunch and lunch options. There's always something veggie or vegan on the menu, and they're dog-friendly too.

ISLAND

Everything on the menu at Island Coffee shop (above) is seriously vibrant and fun. Whether you're after some loaded sourdough toast or a vegan sarnie that will knock your socks off, there are few better places in town for brunch. Grab a forest green smoothie and a colourful granola bowl to get your day off to a good start!

JAM JAR CAFE

Nestled on a quiet corner in the heart of Newquay, this miniature cafe specialises in top notch coffee, using locally roasted beans. There are also superfood smoothies, healthy breakfast bowls and freshly toasted bagels on the menu. All their cakes are freshly baked each day by owner Jess, who also runs The Jam Jar Kitchen over in Crantock village.

EMILY SCOTT FOOD

2021 was a rather good year for chef Emily Scott. As well as publishing a cookbook, she found time to wine and dine the world's political elite at the G7 Summit and opened the doors to her newest venture: Emily Scott Food (below). Perched right by the sea at the idyllic Watergate Bay, this self-titled restaurant follows a less-is-more approach to dining. Guests can expect rustic yet deceptively simple dishes that marry together the land and sea. Just don't expect to get a seat without a reservation - this is one popular spot!

TOM THUMB

Much like Tom Thumb himself, this bar has a legendary reputation. With over 120 bottles of hand chosen spirits – and an untold number of combinations – a night out here guarantees some epic cocktails and good times with friends.

12 BEACH ROAD

This super chilled out restaurant (above) overlooks the iconic Towan Beach and is open all day, from breakfast through to dinner. There's a tempting menu of burgers, tacos and stone-baked sourdough pizza, as well as a great selection of cocktails, wines and craft beers. When your table starts resembling a game of foodie Tetris you know you're onto something good.

THE BOTTLE

The Bottle deli and kitchen was designed to recreate the informal and friendly style of French wine bars. The menu offers a sociable way of dining; with cheese, charcuterie and a variety of sharing boards to enjoy. There's also an eco-friendly refillable wine service with a selection of whites, reds and rosé to buy in anything from 500ml to a litre.

The Island Newquay, Photos by Matthew Heritage

Headland Hotel Cottages

THE ISLAND NEWQUAY

Looking for a totally one-of-a-kind holiday experience? Perched on its very own island, overlooking sandy Towan Beach, you'll find one of the most unique beach houses in all of England: 'The Island' Newquay. This gorgeous holiday home is available to rent through Boutique Retreats and offers unrivalled Atlantic Ocean views and chic interiors throughout. Inside, the house is distinctly New England in style, with a cool colour palette of whites and greys, open plan living and breath-taking vistas from almost every window. You'll reach this magical destination by private footbridge and have the whole island to yourself during your stay.

THE HEADLAND HOTEL COTTAGES

The Headland Hotel's self-catering holiday cottages are set upon a private cliff-top only yards from the sands of Fistral Beach. Aside from the iconic location, each cottage provides guests with a little slice of coastal luxury and plenty of creature comforts. Wake up to the smell of the Atlantic Ocean and curl up on an evening with a glass of fizz and views for miles. Guests also benefit from unlimited use of the Headland's 'five-bubble' rated spa and rosette-worthy restaurant.

MARRIED TO THE SEA

In case the name doesn't make it obvious enough, this clothing shop is dedicated to those who love the ocean. It's a bit of a one-stop shop for anyone looking to hit the beach. Plus, as testament to their sea-loving credentials, Married to the Sea has partnered with Newquay Marine Group to sell graphic tees that promote their hard work protecting the Cornish coastlines.

ROO'S BEACH

Founded by Roo Cross, this fun shop is a Newquay stalwart that bucks the trend of 'coastal' attire. It offers an eclectic and colourful mix of fashion for everyone. You'll find plenty of established brands such as American Vintage, Levi's, Free People and Portuguese Flannel, alongside unique homewares, gorgeous plants and inspiring gifts. But if you've worn yourself out from all that shopping you could always grab a drink and a jam doughnut from their coffee shop!

SAND & PALM

After recognising the need for a more eco-conscious approach to fashion - coupled with years of struggling to find the perfect swimsuit - Vicki Jones (right) founded sustainable swimwear brand: Sand & Palm. Today, her brick-and-mortar shop at Welsey Yard is a chic, calming space filled with beautiful, one-of-a-kind garments. Everything is made in small batches and screen-printed in-house using eco-friendly dyes. Because no two print placements are the same, you can wear your swimsuit with pride knowing it's completely unique to you.

Vicki Jones, founder of
Sand & Palm

Watergate Bay Hotel

newquay

Two miles of golden sand and striking cliffs provide the backdrop to this contemporary beachside hotel. Whether you're paddling out into the surf, lounging by the pool or sipping on cocktails, a stay at Watergate Bay is all about striking the right balance. 'Active relaxation' is the name of the game, so expect plenty of opportunities to get out among the elements, as well as eating and drinking to your heart's content. Rooms at Watergate Bay are effortlessly stylish, with a contemporary coastal aesthetic throughout. For couples, we recommend checking out the luxurious beach lofts; each one boasts immaculate interiors and stunning sea views.

Maverick tip: Head to the Swim Club (Watergate Bay's answer to a spa) and take a dip in the pool or relax in a sea view sauna.

watergatebay.co.uk

Lewinnick Lodge

newquay

Boutique hotel Lewinnick Lodge is perched upon the rugged Pentire headland; well-placed for visiting North Cornwall's iconic surf beaches and for exploring lesser-known spots along the coastline. Being the last building on the cliff, the surrounding sea views feel a bit like they've been designed for the private enjoyment of guests. If blessed with good weather, Lewinnick Lodge also have a terrace that's perfect for soaking up balmy sunsets with a cocktail or two. Although the surrounding salty air might whet your whistle for local seafood (and you wouldn't be disappointed) the restaurant also offers brasserie classics as well. Finish the night off by slipping out of a fluffy robe and into a spacious bathtub that's placed by the window, perfect for contemplating the Atlantic from.

Maverick tip: Lewinnick Lodge is only a stone's throw away from the golden sands of Fistral Beach, so make sure you pack your swimsuit.

lewinnicklodge.co.uk

discover
St Agnes

Curated by Rachæl Brown

Most of us associate St. Agnes with the dramatic ruins of Wheal Coates (left). But the small and thriving community has so much more to offer. The surrounding heathland has been designated an Area of Outstanding Natural Beauty, making for serene walks through sloping hills and cliff tops blanketed in purple and yellow. Nearby you'll find surfers' paradise Porthtowan Beach, and the village of St Agnes itself is home to a variety of independent businesses...

BREAKER'S BEACH CAFE

Location matters. Breaker's Beach Café is built into the cliffs at St. Agnes' beautiful Trevaunance Cove, making the most of its panoramic bay views with big picture windows and serving delicious pasties, cream teas and ice creams to go with it.

THE SORTING OFFICE

Previously a Post Office in the middle of the village, The Sorting Office coffeehouse now lures customers in with the smell of freshly ground coffee beans and a tantalizing array of fresh cakes, including tasty Kernow curls (we'll leave you to discover what these are).

TRUNK DELI

Rummage around Trunk Deli's shelves to find picnic gems: Spanish and Italian produce, craft beer and wine, speciality local ingredients and the best pastrami bagels in all of Cornwall.

SHELLFISH BEACH DELI

This chilled out deli offers all the fresh fruits of the sea; perfect for taking home and transforming into dinner. But if you're too peckish to wait there's a seafood menu in the relaxed restaurant or you can grab a succulent crab roll to take away and enjoy on the beach.

SCHOONERS

Schooners is a laid-back, beachfront restaurant serving an ever changing, seafood-led menu that's big on flavour. Open fired cooking and smoky flavours are high on the agenda, as are craft beers and cocktails. Head here with friends and family to enjoy a delicious offering of small plates and big sharing platters.

CHURCHTOWN ARTS

Churchtown Arts is a real family-run affair. Head here for homewares that reflect St Agnes' calm, coastal lifestyle, as well as gifts for your friends back at home. We're particularly fond of the striped Cornish ware mugs and the fragrant Sea Shed soaps.

MOUNT PLEASANT ECO PARK

Mount Pleasant Eco Park is at the top of the heath-covered valley that concludes in sandy Porthtowan Beach. It offers sustainable wild camping and glamping, with live music in the barn and a large wooden bar that's a temple to local ales, ciders and lagers. Check out Wilder Allotment Kitchen onsite for tasty vegan scran.

KORU KAYAKING

Explore Cornwall's historic coastline with Koru Kayaking, as knowledgeable guides shepherd you to secluded caverns and picturesque bays away from the crowds.

Nancarrow Farm

gelah

Nancarrow is a working organic farm, weddings and events venue nestled in an idyllic hidden valley near Truro. To reach this rural retreat, you must wind your way through a rustic country track lined with old oak trees and ancient Cornish hedgerows, until you reach the heart of the farm. Here, the Nancarrow team has lovingly restored several historic barns to create an inspiring space for gatherings and feasts. There are few better ways to enjoy an evening than to immerse yourself in these beautiful surroundings and experience authentic hospitality from a working farm. The kitchen team specialises in wholesome, home-produced dishes served at the centre of buzzing communal tables.

Maverick tip: Should you wish to extend your stay overnight, Nancarrow offers dinner guests the option to book one of their luxury ensuite bedrooms in the the lovingly restored barn. Alternatively, you could lay your head down in one of the charming shepherds huts positioned in the orchard.

nancarrowfarm.co.uk

The Ugly Butterfly

carbis bay

Chef Adam Handling is no stranger to success. So, when he set his sights on Carbis Bay's golden shores in 2021, we knew we would be in for a treat. The ironically named Ugly Butterfly restaurant is a thoroughly contemporary affair, with huge floor-to-ceiling glass windows looking out over one of the most impressive vistas in Cornwall. However, despite its polished appearance, the restaurant showcases Handling's passion for hyper local food and minimising food waste.

The menu includes intriguing dishes like 'raw and pickled garden vegetables with whipped smoked tofu' or 'Retired dairy cow tartare with girolles and beef fat'. The bar also uses trims and offcuts from leftover ingredients to create delicious drinks and innovative snacks. We're particularly intrigued by the sound of the cheese doughnuts and the waffles with caviar....

Maverick tip: Food is served all day, but for the full experience you should probably opt for one of the tasting menus.

uglybutterfly.co.uk

explore

St Ives

Cobbled streets, impossibly blue waters and a thriving arts scene are all reasons why the town of St Ives is often hailed as the jewel in Cornwall's crown...

EXPLORE ST IVES

Look past the busy summer crowds and tourist hotspots and the town of St Ives has a lot to offer...

There are three main beaches within walking distance of the town centre. **Porthminister Beach** is ideally located for public transport and gives off real Mediterranean vibes during the summer months, thanks to its golden sands and surrounding sub-tropical gardens. The Blue Flag awarded **Porthmeor Beach** is a popular spot for surfers and swimmers alike. It faces the Atlantic Ocean and has lifeguard cover from Easter until the end of October. If you are looking for something a bit more secluded, head to **Porthgwidden Beach**. It's a little tucked away which means it tends to be quieter than its neighbours and is arguably the best spot for families. Overlooked by charming beach huts, it boasts its own restaurant and is a safe spot to paddle in the sea.

For art lovers there are plenty of independent galleries to get your fix. Simply take a wander around the town to experience the myriad of venues on offer, and make sure you pay a visit to the iconic **Tate St Ives** as well. One of the UK's leading galleries, this striking building exhibits work by modern British artists with links to the surrounding area. The Tate gallery also manages the famous **Barbara Hepworth Museum and Sculpture Garden**, which was once the home and studio of the late 20th-century sculptor.

To see St Ives from a different angle, head to the harbour and hop on a boat. Whether you like the sound of a fast rib ride or you would prefer to take a scenic ride along the coast to spy local seals, there are few better ways to spend an afternoon and to sample good old-fashioned Cornish hospitality.

there are three main beaches within walking distance of town

SHOPPING IN ST IVES

Don't be fooled by its touristy credentials. St Ives is home to a myriad of independent shops that sell everything from plush homewares to intricate jewellery...

As its name suggests, **The St Ives Company** is a homegrown lifestyle boutique on Fore Street that's filled with all manner of gifts and treats from nearby makers and businesses. Established by three local sisters, Tegen, Ainslie and Safi, the concept behind the store is to allow visitors to take a little piece of St Ives home with them from their travels. You'll find everything from soy wax candles and scented bath salts to art prints, ceramics and cleverly curated homewares. There's also the opportunity to build your own Cornish hampers.

A few doors along you'll find **St Ives Bakery**: a very photogenic little shop that's brimming with freshly-baked goodies. They've got a particular penchant for pasties and their artisan breads are brilliant. The window is usually stacked high with all manner of tasty things, including fluffy pink meringues and delicate Portuguese custard tarts.

You'll find **The Painted Bird** at Market Place at the end of St Ives' main shopping street. They showcase a collection of carefully chosen products for the home, body and living. It's a celebration of all things handmade, natural and unique; with shelves that are filled with products both beautiful and useful. Head here for vegan leather purses, elegant silver jewellery and delicate dried flowers.

Nestled among St Ives' art galleries and backstreet bistros is the effortlessly charming **Magpie & London**. We love their selection of women's accessories, including cosy cashmere socks and unique crescent moon jewellery – and their musical taste is usually on point too!

The Allotment Deli sources all its produce as locally as possible, priding themselves on their Cornish credentials and supporting local brands. The shop is full of colourful produce and tasty treats to take away, including freshly made sandwiches, salads and fresh vegetable tarts.

WHERE TO EAT IN ST IVES

Porthminster Café is our first port of call for beachside dining in St Ives. This award-winning restaurant brings together the flavours of Asia and the Mediterranean, with dishes such as fragrant Indonesian monkfish curry and sticky pork belly with kimchi and cashew cream. Although not exclusively a fish restaurant, its prime location on the golden sands of Porthminster beach lends itself to putting seafood at centre stage.

When date night's calling, we recommend booking a table at **The Cellar Bistro**. This cosy and relaxed restaurant comes highly recommended by locals, partly due to the fabulous cooking but also the warm and unpretentious service. Look forward to hearty portions of food with a nod to the classics, all washed down with a menu of good-value wine and cocktails.

Another hidden gem is **Mermaid Seafood Restaurant**, which is rather appropriately located on Fish Street. Décor is something of a throwback - with fairy lights strung in the rafters and red gingham tablecloths - but the restaurant is all the more charming for it. Here you'll find legendary seafood platters alongside tempting daily specials (which includes locally caught lobster during the summer months).

Elsewhere in town, we love **The Searoom** by the harbour side for tapas and drinks with friends. Established by the creators of St Ives Gin, there's plenty of imaginative cocktails to choose from as well as tasty small plates of punchy flavours.

STAY IN ST IVES

Newly renovated **Onda** is a chic apartment in the centre of town with lighthouse views and swoon-worthy interiors. A cool coastal colour palette of blues and icy whites runs throughout the property, while underfloor heating and plush 100-thread-count bedding ensures a cosy stay during the winter months.

The Lobster Residence is a boutique cottage by the sea that comfortably sleeps five. Step through the pink Dutch door and you'll be greeted by fun and homely interiors, as well as everything you could need for a relaxing family holiday. The cottage is dog-friendly (just check out their own adorable pooch on Instagram) and perfectly positioned for rambles on Porthmeor Beach.

Another boutique venue in town is the beautiful **Harbourview House**. Rooms at this guesthouse are simple yet chic, and their onsite café and bar is a wonderful place to kick back with a coffee and enjoy the view. Guests can make use of free parking during their stay and look forward to a complimentary drink and freshly made breakfast in the morning.

Nearby **Carbis Bay Hotel** needs no introduction. While technically not located in St Ives town, this luxurious coastal retreat boasts a privately owned 25-acre Blue Flag beach, state-of-the-art spa facilities and some seriously enviable views across one of the world's most beautiful bays. If you're happy to part with some cash, book one of their new beach lodges and an evening at The Ugly Butterfly Restaurant for an unforgettable trip.

When in doubt about where to stay, check out local bookings agency, **So St Ives**. Their portfolio of properties contains everything from family-friendly cottages to stylish apartments that are perfect for couples.

HOST

st ives

Housed in a former bank, HOST offers two sensationally designed suites for a little slice of luxury in the heart of St Ives. Choose between the opulent Terrace Suite or the equally luxe Library Suite – both of which offer secure underground parking nearby.

The Terrace Suite is an expansive open plan living space with its own private south facing terrace. Sleep soundly in a super king size bed, with plush savoy bedding, or soak away your stresses in the Catchpole & Rye bespoke roll top bathtub. Complimentary toiletries come courtesy of The White Company's Noir Collection and snuggly robes will be waiting for you when you can finally tear yourself away from the tub. In The Library Suite you can stretch out on an extra-large, sumptuous sofa with a drink in hand and your favourite book for company. Whatever the Cornish weather has in store, both suites benefit from underfloor heating and air conditioning. Rooms offer views of historic Tregenna Hill, while the walls host stunning original artwork by local artists.

Maverick tip: HOST's generously stocked butler's station is brimming with Cornish artisan delicacies, including locally roasted coffee from Origin Coffee, craft beers and local spirits.

hoststives.co.uk

The Library Suite at HOST, Photos by Nik Read

Tremenheere
Sculpture Gardens

Penzance

In a sheltered valley near Penzance, you'll find a truly one-of-a-kind attraction: Tremenheere Sculpture Gardens. Once a neglected woodland, today the gardens are a feat of landscaping, where structured shrubs frame painting-like vistas of the iconic St. Michael's Mount. Cushioned by the surrounding hillsides and warmed by a mild sea breeze, Tremenheere benefits from its own unique microclimate.

Large scale exotic and sub-tropical planting provide the backdrop to inspiring art by internationally renowned artists, such as James Turrell, David Nash and Richard Long. Each artist has interacted with the setting to create site specific, permeant work that harmonises with the landscape. Tremenheere is also home to a state-of-the-art gallery. With two exhibition spaces spread across two floors, this beautiful oak framed building attracts the very best creative talent from far and wide. Since opening in January 2017, it has hosted solo exhibitions by several revered artists, including Gillian Ayres, Romi Behrens, and Jessica Cooper.

Maverick tip: Tremenheere also boasts is own garden nursery, gift shop and café (where you'll find an ever-evolving menu and seriously great views).

tremenheere.co.uk

discover

Penzance

Written by Sophie Farrah

Tucked in the rugged far west of Cornwall, the vibrant market
town of Penzance has it all. Coastal views, beautiful
architecture, a thriving art scene and fantastic food to boot.
This historic port offers eccentric charm in bucketloads, and
whilst it may be the very last stop on the old Great Western
train line, it's definitely worth the journey.

ARTISTIC LICENSE

Enticed by the coastal landscapes and famous light, artists have flocked to West Cornwall since the early 1880s. The Newlyn Art Gallery was established to display works from the famous Newlyn School, but today the focus is on world-class contemporary art. In the heart of Penzance, The Exchange is the gallery's second modern art venue, and the nearby Penlee House Gallery & Museum, with its sub-tropical gardens, is another scenic spot to discover local art and the town's fascinating history.

Just outside the main town, art and nature combine in glorious harmony at Tremenheere Sculpture Garden; this beautiful valley, complete with woods, stream and incredible views, is a picture-perfect setting for exotic plants interwoven with contemporary art installations (and a great café too). Finally, if you feel like letting your own creative juices flow, head to Newlyn School of Art where you can enrol on a painting course taught by some of the most well-known artists working in Cornwall today.

GET ACTIVE

A dip in the Art Deco spectacle that is Jubilee Pool is a must; this iconic spot is the UK's largest seawater lido, and it hangs over the sea. Enjoy the views from one of its terraces or do some laps in the main pool before enjoying a soak in the toasty, geothermally heated section. New electric bike rental company E Bike Cornwall offers a fun and easy way to explore the area; either head off on your own with one of the ingenious sat navs (pre-loaded with several routes) or zip along the Promenade and coastal path on a guided tour, learning about local history along the way.

FOOD GLORIOUS FOOD

The hottest table in town is at The Shore; an intimate little restaurant with a supper club vibe run by accomplished chef Bruce Rennie who creates all the dishes himself, from the incredible bread and butter through to delicate dishes using local fish, meat and vegetables from nearby growers.

Just a short amble along the seafront is historic maritime pub The Tolcarne Inn, where chef Ben Tunnicliffe's chalkboard menu offers fresh seafood (pictured top left) from nearby Newlyn Harbour expertly combined with locally sourced ingredients. Seafood lovers should also visit the newly opened Argoe; a trendy spot with minimalist interiors, natural wines and a gorgeous harbour side terrace. Set up by Penzance local Rich Adams, the menu here prioritises freshness over familiarity, featuring under-appreciated species like megrim sole and horse mackerel.

Excellent coffee can be found at Lovetts, which also serves a mean Sunday brunch (think Bloody Marys and kimchi cheese toasties) and operates as a welcoming wine bar by night, serving natural and low-intervention bottles with tasty small plates. 45 Queen Street is another cool café, bar and event space housed in an old warehouse, recently opened by organic Cornish gin Tinkture's founder, Hannah Lamiroy. Pop in for coffee, fabulous cakes, seasonal food and delicious cocktails.

The best pasties in town can be found at The Cornish Hen; a dreamy deli filled with all manner of artisanal treats. For award-winning fish and chips head to Fraser's, widely considered some of the best in Cornwall, let alone Penzance. And if you've still got room, don't miss the ice cream at Jelberts, one of the oldest ice cream makers in the county. There's only one flavour – traditional vanilla – made to a top-secret recipe...

CHECK IN

With its beautiful mix of Georgian style, modern architecture and contemporary comfort, Chapel House is one of our favourite places to stay. It has six spacious double rooms and two splendid suites, all bathed in natural light and offering sea views, bespoke oak beds and wow factor bathrooms. Downstairs, there's an elegant drawing room adorned with Cornish art, a pretty garden and relaxed dining room, where owner Susan whips up all manner of feasts, from breakfast and brunches through to informal weekend suppers using the best local produce.

DON'T MISS

Finally, no trip to Penzance would be complete without a visit to St Michael's Mount. This fairy-tale tiny island is crowned by a medieval church and castle, with the oldest buildings dating from the 12th century. Take a short boat ride to the island or, at low tide, walk across the rocky causeway and enjoy the breath-taking views of Mount's Bay.

RETAIL THERAPY

It's impossible to leave Penzance empty handed. Chapel Street is lined with arty independent shops and hidden amongst the town's cobbled alleyways you'll find an array of antiques, collectables, curios and more. We love the cool, coastal tones of No.56, a beautifully designed spot filled with natural products for the modern home. Circa 21 is a treasure trove of ethical, locally made homeware and gifts, and for unique furniture finds head to Daisy Laing; this art gallery and home emporium is brimming with treasures, including an ever-changing collection of vintage and mid-century modern furniture.

The Alverton Hotel

Truro

Cocooned on the outskirts of Truro, you'll discover a gorgeous, ivy-clad hotel steeped in history and verdant landscapes. Once a Cornish convent, The Alverton has earned Grade II listed status, and its breathtaking architecture is a sight to behold. But, step through its impressive oak doors and you'll be just as enamoured with the twenty-first century offerings...

Each of the hotel's 51 bedrooms honour the rich history of The Alverton, with original characteristics such as brick exposed feature walls, antique furniture and wooden paneling. For added indulgence, opt to stay in the romantic Bishop Suite with its double roll-top bath tubs; or book a stay in the lavish Chapel Suite with its vaulted ceilings, stained glass windows and plush bedding.

At The Alverton's award-winning restaurant you'll savour Cornish-inspired cuisine, served by Head Chef Erkki Mikk. Erkki's passion for rich local ingredients is evident in his beautifully presented dishes that are a feast for the eyes and the taste buds. Menus change with the seasons to showcase the very best of the south west. So fuel up on heart-warming classics, unforgettable puddings and inventive culinary creations.

Elsewhere, you can sip on hand-crafted cocktails overlooking the gardens, indulge in bottomless gin brunches or make yourself at home by the fire. Whatever you choose, let The Alverton bring a slice of country living to your stay in the city.

thealverton.co.uk

visit
Truro

The cathedral city of Truro is often dubbed the unofficial 'capital of Cornwall'. From art galleries to hidden indie gems, it's a quiet and quaint labyrinth of hidden streets ripe for exploration. Potter around its cobbled lanes, roam its weekly markets, and discover the many shops and eateries that call this city home...

LAWRANCE'S BAKERY & BAR

This blush-pink bakery and bar serves a range of cakes, brownies and blondies, along with warm petal-sprinkled pastries and smoothies in various pastel shades (including blue!). Enjoy perfectly poured coffees during the day or head back on an evening for colourful cake-based cocktails. Lawrence's really is the perfect place for those who love sweet treats.

POLLEN

Endearingly known as the 'thoughtful snackery', Pollen is a largely plant-based café, offering eco-conscious breakfasts and beverages. It's a calming spot, perfect for munching on a bagel or catching up with friends over a tasty chai pot. If you can, try to get your hands on one of their popular glazed doughnuts - they fly off the shelves like literal hot cakes.

LILY'S OF TRURO

The unusual and delicious cruffins – a hybrid of a muffin and a croissant - that crowd the counter at Lily's of Truro really say something about the place itself; it's quirky and comforting, yet oh so creative. Lily's is a great place to stop for vegan cakes, healthy breakfasts and fresh juices after a spot of retail therapy.

SABZI DELI

Sabzi Deli offers a plentiful selection of fresh, seasonal fare to take away that is bursting with Middle Eastern flavours. Inside you'll be greeted by large bowls of colourful, freshly chopped vegetables, salad leaves and fluffy couscous that are heavy on citrus, spices and herby flavours. They also serve plenty of nourishing hot dhals for a sunny, hearty lunch that packs a real punch.

Longstore Brunch, Photo by Frankie Thomas

THE LONGSTORE AT LEMON STREET

Housed in a renovated Georgian townhouse, The Longstore at Lemon Street specialise in big cuts of dry-aged steak, seafood dishes, and a punchy range of bar bites to snack on with your cocktails. It's a unique blend of city dining with warm and welcoming service to boot.

HOOKED!

It wouldn't be a Cornish guide without mentioning a brilliant seafood spot. The talented chefs at this laid-back restaurant and bar revolve their menu around the latest catch from Cornish waters, and are massively popular for it. Expect ingredients like Falmouth scallops, local mussels and Cornish lobster.

TRURO COOKERY SCHOOL

Truro Cookery School is all about the act of making and sharing food together. Enjoy a relaxed evening learning how to cook with your friends and sip on a glass of fizz whilst you watch expert chefs demo their signature dishes. You're welcome to bring your own booze and you'll come away with plenty of new skills - all without having to do any of the washing up!

THE RISING SUN

You'll find lots of fresh Cornish ingredients on the menu at popular local venue The Rising Sun (above). This award-winning country pub produces high-quality, creative plates, all served in a cosy, convivial atmosphere. What's more, it's also dog-friendly.

the perfect pit stop after a day
spent shopping!

HALL FOR CORNWALL

Catch everything from international tours and stand up comedy, to orchestral performances at this lively arts venue. The Hall for Cornwall auditorium has recently been transformed to hold over 1000 seats, making it the best place in town to soak up a little culture.

HESELTINE GALLERY

For an inspiring afternoon, we suggest a trip to Truro's Heseltine Gallery. Here you can pore over a mixture of paintings, sculpture and mixed media art. The gallery regularly hosts curated exhibitions featuring work from young artists and the local creative community. There's also an intriguing collection of work from influential artists such as Sir Terry Frost and Cornwall's very own Jeremy Le Grice.

UNEEKA

Independent business Uneeka focuses on locally sourced furniture, antiques and homewares – all ethically selected. Here you can find all the artistic flourishes that give character to a room; we'd recommend putting aside some time for browsing those touches of colour and texture. There's also a lovely café upstairs that is the perfect pit stop after a day spent shopping.

DA BARA IN THE GARDEN

This next joint is not strictly speaking in the centre of Truro, but it's worth seeking it out. You'll find Da Bara in the Garden in a giant outdoor tipi in the peaceful Roseland Plant Centre. Look out for their staples: sugar dusted cinnamon buns, artisan bread, coffee and cakes. It's a charming spot for an outdoor breakfast.

Slice of Cornwall, Photo by Jack Farmer

Slice of Cornwall

constantine

Not far from Falmouth is the lovely Trewardreva Mill in Constantine. Here you'll find 'Slice of Cornwall' a popular eatery that serves some of the best brunch offerings in the county. The venue itself is located in a beautiful spot hidden amongst the greenery, with plenty of outdoor seating and ample parking. Meanwhile, inside is a contemporary, laid-back space, with lofty ceilings and a thoroughly modern bar.

With a menu that offers everything from tasty breakfast waffles to huevos rancheros, there's bound to be something to take your fancy. There's also plenty of tempting dishes for vegans and veggies, and coffee ranges from the classic flat white to gingerbread lattes and hazelnut mochas.

Maverick tip: When in doubt, order the waffles. They've got their very own section of the menu and they arrive piled high on your plate with original toppings such as smoked salmon or fried chicken.

sliceofcornwall.com

Mistery 2

nr falmouth

Hidden along the banks of the River Kennall you'll find this extraordinary houseboat that's perfect for your next Cornish adventure. Mistery 2 is a one-of-a-kind hideaway that has been lovingly renovated by owners Mark and Loz. The couple have gone to great lengths to source and transform recycled materials to craft the boats unique interiors and magical outdoor space.

Inside, you'll find two tastefully decorated bedrooms (or cabins), a rather snug bathroom, a fully equipped kitchen and a living / dining space complete with a log burner for nights spent cosied up inside. Outside, the garden space is almost as impressive as the boathouse herself. Set within two acres of land, green pastures and river views provide the backdrop to your stay. Sit by the compass fire-pit and sip on G&Ts or enjoy a friendly chit chat with the resident chickens.

Maverick tip: The internet is a little patchy, so be prepared for a bit of a digital detox during your stay. You can always make the most of your direct access to the river for paddling or kayaking (just be aware of tide times).

Book via Unique Hideaways:
uniquehideaways.com

24 hours in

Falmouth

The coastal town of Falmouth truly is a one-of-a-kind destination. It's home to many of Cornwall's most exciting indie brands and a university that has produced some of the UK's finest artistic talent. Its vibrant streets are often festooned with colourful bunting and its sandy beaches rival their North Coast cousins. So, whether you're after a boutique getaway or a weekend full of culture, Falmouth is bound to have something to offer.

TREBAH GARDENS

Falmouth is surrounded by beautiful public gardens, including Trelissick, Enys and Glendurgan; but the sub-tropical paradise of Trebah Gardens should be at the top of your go-to list. Open to the public year round, this 26-acre Cornish valley garden is only a 15-minute drive from Falmouth town centre and contains over four miles of footpath to explore. In spring, the gardens come alive with a colourful array of 100-year-old rhododendrons, while in autumn Hydrangea Valley blossoms into floral clouds of china blue and soft white hues. Whatever the season, don't miss Trebah's very own secluded beach down on the Helford River.

PENDENNIS CASTLE

History buffs should make their way to Pendennis Castle - a mighty fortress built by Henry VIII which later played a vital role during the two World Wars. Today, English Heritage maintains the historic site, offering visitors the opportunity to be transported back in time and learn about the landmark's unique and important past. Located at Pendennis Point, visitors can climb to the top of the castle keep and scan the horizon for enemies (while simultaneously enjoying the picturesque coastal views).

GYLLYNGVASE BEACH

This golden beach is a great place to throw down your towel and take a dip in the sea. With RNLI Lifeguard cover between May and September and minimal rip currents, it's a safe beach for families and novice swimmers. WeSUP (stand up paddle board centre) and Gylly Adventures can get you on the water in no time with equipment hire and expert tuition. There are also plenty of amenities to enjoy, with the fabulous Gylly Beach Cafe open year round, offering food, drink and live music.

SWANPOOL BEACH

If you like the sound of an afternoon spent kayaking, then Swanpool Beach is the place to go. Visitors can rent a kayak for as little as £10 an hour and the sheltered bay makes Swanpool the perfect place for beginners to learn. Wade into its calm blue waters and explore the surrounding coastline from a whole new perspective.

STAR GLAZEY POTTERY CAFE

Embrace your inner artist at Star Glazey pottery café – the only place in town where you can paint your own ceramic creation with a cup of tea in hand. This buzzing venue on Falmouth High Street is usually filled with talented arty types and families looking to unleash their creativity. They also offer personalised gifts such as clay imprints, glazed footprints and fingerprint jewellery - the perfect way to capture a moment in time.

BEERWOLF BOOKS

We're big fans of puns, so with a name like Beerwolf Books this next venue was already onto a winner. It's a pub meets bookshop (yes, you read that correctly) tucked away at the top of an alley that leads off Market Street. With its mock Tudor façade and shelves brimming with books, it's a big hit with students and locals alike and remains something of a hidden gem. The atmosphere is seriously relaxed, so buy a book and sit down with a pint or make the most of their free-to-use board games.

a great place to throw down your
towel & take a dip!

THE FALMOUTH BOOKSELLER

Falmouth Bookseller is an independent bookshop on Church Street that stocks everything from the hottest new fiction to cookbooks and local interest titles. Head here for regular book signings and meet-the-author events. The shop also decides on the reading list for 'The Upstairs Downstairs Book Group', who meet once a month to drink tea or sip on gin as they chat about their latest read.

INSPIRE MAKERS

Inspire Makers is a new creative space on Falmouth High Street that showcases the talent of more than fifty Cornish design-led arts and craftspeople. Browse affordable work from well-known and emerging makers, including one-of-a-kind jewellery, ceramics, textiles, wall art, stationery and homewares. You can read the story behind each maker, giving you an insight into what inspires them and drives their creativity. The best part? Buying handcrafted work supports small, creative businesses and means you'll have something truly unique to appreciate for years to come.

THE BEAN HIVE BY THE SEA

Fun and colourful are just two of the words that spring to mind when you step into this next shop. Self-described as 'beigephobic' this quirky pink shop lives by the mantra of 'more is more'. Lovers of bold and eccentric designs will no doubt pick up something fabulous to take home among the quirky cushions, decorations and stationery.

BOTANICAL ATELIER

We're big fans of the beautiful Botanical Atelier on Arwenack Street. Founder Sarah Jane Humphrey is a talented botanical illustrator and all-around taste maker. Through Botanical Atelier she brings together her talents with a beautiful collection of homewares and botanically inspired products. Swoon over her painstakingly detailed drawings and browse the many art materials, prints and homewares on display. Sarah also runs regular classes from the shop, teaching students how to master their own botanical drawings and paintings.

HIGHCLIFFE B&B

Highcliffe B&B is perfectly located for exploring everything Falmouth has to offer. Only a five-minute walk into the town centre and a stone's throw away from the beachfront, its boutique credentials and eight gorgeous rooms have earned it an enviable reputation. Choose a room that best suits your style, from the spacious penthouse suite to cosy bolt holes with king size beds and creature comforts. Come morning, you can indulge in your very own breakfast picnic, complete with everything from bacon and eggs to pancake stacks and homemade granola.

THE SANDY DUCK

It's not ordinary practice for a B&B to offer guests super-king beds and freestanding baths. But then again, The Sandy Duck isn't exactly an 'ordinary' B&B. Each of its eight impeccably designed bedrooms contain the perfect ingredients for a good night's sleep: Egyptian cotton sheets, luxurious bathrooms and nourishing Land & Water toiletries. Also bucking B&B norms is The Sandy Duck's lounge - a light flooded space to unwind in summer or cosy up in winter where a roaring fire awaits you.

THE STAR & GARTER

We can't get enough of this restaurant with rooms on Falmouth High Street. With an award-winning restaurant on its ground floor and three beautifully designed apartments upstairs, The Star & Garter brings together good food, good design and good vibes. All three suites are fabulous, but we recommend booking The Crows Nest for uninterrupted views over Falmouth harbour and your very own log burner during the colder months. Downstairs, the Sunday roast is pretty legendary (as are the beautiful, blue views from the restaurant's picture windows).

MERCHANTS MANOR

This next hotel prides itself on being a thoroughly 'grownup getaway' and it's not hard to see why. Home to a three-rosette restaurant, some stunning residences and a wellness spa, Merchants Manor ticks plenty of boxes for a romantic getaway. From experience, you'll want to upgrade to one of the Original House Rooms during your stay and sample chef Hylton's fine dining menu in the bright and stylish Rastella restaurant.

Highcliffe B&B, Photo by Lizzie Churchill

Merchant Manor's Landlubber Residency

INDIdog, Photo by Lizzie Churchill

INDIDOG

Over the years INDIdog has earned some serious bragging rights for its stunning water views and delicious breakfasts. If you can nab yourselves a table, we suggest tucking into a fluffy stack of pancakes or trying the best omelette in town — honestly, they swear by it! Alternatively, hit INDIdog on an evening for some quality Cornish fare.

VERDANT SEAFOOD BAR

The clue is in the name — this cosy taproom serves some mighty good seafood tapas and is situated close to the water on Quay Street. Expect small plates featuring amazingly fresh fish, along with eight lines of beer from Verdant's own artisanal brewery. Of course, there's also beer curated from some of the best breweries in the world. Walk-ins only.

MINE, Photos by Emily Marco Vecchio

RESTAURANT MINE

This intimate neighbourhood restaurant spills out onto the cobbles of The Old Brewery Yard and is fast gaining a reputation as one of Falmouth's finest foodie establishments. Chef Angus Bell oversees a menu of simple, playful dishes made with ingredients from Cornwall's finest producers – all washed down with a concise yet considered wine list.

HOOKED ON THE ROCKS

You'll need to travel a little out of town to reach this beachside bistro. Hooked on the Rocks specialises in freshly caught seafood dishes (see above) and seasonal craft cocktails. Outside, the sun-drenched terrace is the perfect spot to look out across Swanpool beach and nature reserve. Inside, décor is unexpectedly lavish, with a rich colour palette, comfy velvet chairs and intimate booth seating.

THE WHEELHOUSE

You'll need to book a table far in advance if you want to eat at this extremely popular restaurant. Set away from the main thoroughfare on Upton Slip, you won't miss the bright and colourful signage for The Wheelhouse. Sat right on the water, seafood is their speciality with super-fresh scallops, oysters and lobster regularly making an appearance on the menu. Décor is rustic and full of character, with wooden beams, stone floors and dripping candles. There's nothing pretentious about this warm and welcoming venue and nor does there need to be, as the food speaks for itself.

Kona Bar, Photo by Elliot Eastman

KONA BAR

It's not every day that you get to eat authentic Hawaiian food in Cornwall, but at Kona Bar you can experience the 'beers, bowls and beats' of the tropical paradise. You'll find Kona in the heart of Events Square overlooking Pendennis Harbour, where you can pull up a chair outside or sit in their vibrant tiki-style restaurant. Menus showcase the best of Hawaii and Cornwall, with curries and local seafood high on the agenda and colourful poké bowls stealing the show. To top it off there's also a cocktail menu featuring tipples like frozen margaritas and Polynesian rum punch.

ESPRESSINI

Coffee aficionados will wax lyrical about this tiny independent coffee house at 39 Killigrew Street. Expect hand-roasted espresso blends and single estate coffee from the cream of speciality roasters. If you're travelling with a coffee snob there's nowhere better in town, plus they serve some rather tasty brunch options if you fancy making a morning of it.

The Greenbank Hotel

falmouth

Perched on Falmouth's harbour overlooking the Carrick Roads, The Greenbank is the seaside town's oldest hotel, dating back to the 1600s. This premier venue oozes contemporary elegance and offers a relaxed luxury experience to all guests and visitors.

When it comes to comfort and character, The Greenbank's stylish rooms have it all. From views to stop you in your tracks, to wide-headed showers that you won't want to leave; even the smallest details have been taken care of so you can get lost in your stay.

Feeling adventurous? There are few better ways to experience life on the water than by stepping out of your room and straight on to a waiting boat. The Greenbank is the only hotel in the south west with its own private pontoons, so you can be on the water in no time.

Alongside the bobbing boats and mesmerising maritime scenery, the Water's Edge restaurant is an idyllic spot for fantastic seafood and inventive dishes created with Cornish flair by Head Chef Bobby Southworth.

Knowledgeable waiting staff are always on hand to guide you through the day's specials, while a carefully selected wine list will tempt you with perfectly matched bottles to complement the menu. Searching for a cocktail night with a difference? The bar also offers a unique range of handcrafted cocktails and mocktails that blend together the finest spirits and local ingredients.

The Water's Edge restaurant, bar and terrace serve food all day until late, so you're welcome to arrive at a time that suits you. All you need to do is relax, enjoy and drink in those stunning water views.

www.greenbank-hotel.co.uk

THE
WORKING
-BOAT-

Smooth brews, harbour views and heartfelt food. At The Working Boat, they're all about taking things easy and making the most of life on the water. Established in 1876 and rebuilt in 2015, many a Cornish pint has been sipped on the premises and this cosy little pub by the harbour honours the rich history deeply engrained in Falmouth's sea-faring past.

The beer flows as freely as the chatter and laughter amongst old friends catching up over a few swift drinks, while pub grub is thoughtfully prepared by the kitchen crew and served up in hearty portions to keep the hunger at bay and satisfy the taste buds. The heart of the pub lies in the community and there is never a dull day down by the harbour.

Greenbank Quay, Harbourside, Falmouth, TR11 2SR | theworkingboat.co.uk | 01326 314 283

  @theworkingboat

The Idle Rocks

st mawes

The Idle Rocks is located on the Roseland Peninsula in the heart of St Mawes, an idyllic spot voted as the best seaside town in the UK. Anchoring St Mawes' reputation as a desirable Cornish location, this small hotel is considered one of the region's top luxury retreats. All the interiors – which were designed by hotel owner Karen Richards – incorporate traditional coastal culture and contemporary design. The restaurant, led by former Le Manoir chef Dorian Janmaat, focuses on locally sourced produce with flavour, texture and presentation being integral to all dishes. Uniquely positioned on the water, the hotel gives guests access to a multitude of activities, including sailing, walking or fishing.

Maverick tip: Tucked away on the upper floor of the hotel, you'll find The Reef Knot Retreat Treatment Room. Here you can book an array of wellness treatments, from full body massages to invigorating facials.

idlerocks.com

Malmo

perranwortha

In a creekside hamlet near the river Kennall, you'll find
Malmo. This light and bright converted stable block with
Scandi-inspired décor is the brainchild of interior
designers Becca and Heather, who came together to
create something very special. Malmo is close to the
beaches and cobbled streets of Falmouth, whilst also
being within easy reach of the north coast. The house
sleeps four with one large double bedroom, a smaller twin
room and two luxuriously renovated bathrooms. Upstairs,
you'll find the living space and kitchen, sharing a stunning
double-height space with beamed ceilings and a unique,
reclaimed wood feature wall. Huge original sash windows
flood the space with light throughout the day and guests
can hunker down in one of two comfy windows seats
filled with handmade linen and grain sack cushions.
Alternatively, curl up on the enormous L-shaped sofa and
flick through stacks of magazines or coffee table books.

Maverick tip: Head through the French doors off the
bedroom into a pretty walled courtyard garden, perfect for
enjoying your morning coffee or an evening glass of wine.

Book via Sawdays:
sawdays.co.uk

The Cob Barn

nr st austell

If you really want to feel like you're living the romantic countryside dream, you could do worse than to wake up in the renovated Cob Barn, collect eggs from their friendly hens and rustle up a tasty breakfast in the farmhouse kitchen. Placed quite centrally in Cornwall, The Cob Barn allows guests to easily explore different corners of the county but is closest to lovely Porthpean beach and St. Austell.

The building itself was affectionately restored using traditional Cornish methods and timber from Plymouth dockyards. It's quiet and rustic but uncompromising on comfort, with a wet room shower, heated slate flooring and a projector for film nights. Lots of walking paths criss-cross through the surrounding countryside for rambling types, but if you fancy sticking nearby there's outdoor seating in their tranquil yard. There's one bedroom but two additional beds can be set up to accommodate four guests in total.

Maverick tip: Make use of the nearby bridle path that joins to the National Cycle Trail. It'll take you to Pentewan Sands along the beautiful Pentewan Valley Trail avoiding roads.

thecobbarn.com

Visit Charlestown

The heart of Charlestown is its historic port, where white washed cottages overlook the harbour and the tall masts of wooden boats hint at the villages' Georgian past. Charlestown is a popular filming location, so take a stroll along its quaint streets and you'll spy scenery straight out of Poldark.

SPRINGTIDE

Charlestown's newest seafood restaurant boasts a tempting menu of lobster, oysters and fresh fish on a daily basis. They serve dinner 7 nights a week and there's a lovely outdoor terrace with unrivalled harbour views for sunny days.

SHORT & STRONG

Brunch spot Short & Strong offers a wonderful selection of cakes and pastries. They also serve some excellent toasties on a lunchtime; so head upstairs to the restaurant or pull up a chair outside under the sunlit blue parasols.

THE WINESTORE

The Winestore have a well-stocked cellar full of interesting bottles from small producers, but we also love its tapas and small plate offerings. Served in a cosy ambience, they're the perfect pairing for wine tasting by the glass.

THE LONGSTORE

Expect to find bold flavours at The Longstore Charlestown. This restaurant specialises in fresh Cornish seafood and hefty dry-aged steaks, with the option of the local butcher's cut specifically chosen by the chef on the day. They're also known for their exceedingly good cocktails. If you're looking for a more cosmopolitan vibe with an easy-going Cornish ambience, this is the place to be.

SLEEP ON A CLASSIC SHIP

Anny is a charming 1930's classic sailing ship moored in Charlestown Harbour. Fully heated and very comfortable, Anny provides unique accommodation for up to eight in a historic setting. Once you've sampled life aboard, you may want to test your sea legs for real. Ask about upcoming day sails and cruises on this stunning vessel. Book through Air B&B or directly via charlestownharbour.com

SET SAIL!

Synonymous with its classic tall ships, Charlestown harbour offers thrill seekers the opportunity to explore the local waters on a traditional, working vessel. From a 3 hour day trip to a 3 day voyage, discover your inner sailor and take in the remarkable views of the beautiful South coast.

Marine Villa, Antonia's Pearls

ANTONIA'S PEARLS

Antonia's Pearls are a collection of luxurious seaside cottages and villas dotted around Charlestown. They're decorated to feel like cosy hideaways, with wood burning stoves, private seaside gardens and impeccable interiors. They also have extremely close access to the surrounding harbour and beaches, making them ideal boltholes for your holiday.

CHARLESTOWN BEACH

Charlestown has a quiet beach that backs onto the village. Its shoreline is pebbly and a calming grey, which often means that it's not as crowded as some spots can get in Cornwall. Make like a smuggler and head through the tunnel to the sea for a refreshing dip.

The Eden Project

bodelva

When Tim Smit first conceived The Eden Project it was hailed as an ambitious and highly imaginative concept; and twenty years later, the ecological marvel continues to ignite the imaginations of both the young and old. Stepping through the first waft of humidity in the rainforest biome (left) rouses all the senses, as there's something seriously inspiring about the sheer scale of its jungle canopies. Couple this experience with the sights and scents of the Mediterranean biome – as well as large scale art installations throughout – and you've got the perfect recipe for an unforgettable family day out. We'd also recommend the adrenaline spiking adventure activities on site with Hangloose Eden. You can experience thrilling bungee drops, send yourself flying on a giant swing or shoot over the domes and past chalk cliffs on England's fastest zip wire.

Maverick tip: Don't neglect their cultural events or Eden Sessions either. There's everything from light shows to live music on the agenda, with some household names on the events calendar!

edenproject.com

24 hours in

Mevagissey

Made famous for its pilchard fishing, the coastal village of Mevagissey is a tightly woven knot of old pubs, independent shops and seafood restaurants that circle around the water. Here's our pick for things to do when you're visiting for a weekend...

TASTE THE LOCAL FARE

Being on the seafront and in a thriving fishing port, we'd make a beeline for Mevagissey harbour to taste-test the local catch. The Fish Grill & More is a popular food truck open in the summer season, serving fresh seafood (and not just of the battered variety). Think plump scallops, tasty mackerel or swordfish and chips. For battered cod year-round, The Fisherman's Chippy is a classic. And for authentic Portuguese food, restaurant Alvorada is the perfect spot.

PADDLE IN POLSTREATH

It's easy to be seduced by Mevagissey's beautiful harbour but if you stray just 15 minutes down the coastal path, you'll find Polstreath beach (pictured left). On a sunny day the water there is like sea glass, pure and clear, lapping onto the shingle shore. It's also sheltered, so good for paddling. A word of caution: the steps down are steep!

WANDER THE NARROW STREETS

Mevagissey is a great place to potter around in. Its winding streets are also a good opportunity for light shopping. You'll find it delightfully Cornish in what it offers: galleries, artisan gifts and the occasional fudge shop. We recommend heading to popular spot She Sells for crêpes, coffee and bagels.

The Pilchard Press

Mevagissey

The Pilchard Press is a private apartment, housed in a whitewashed cottage just a few steps from Mevagissey quayside. It sleeps two in a comfortable king bed and has all the equipment you need for cooking a quiet meal in and watching a film in the cosy lounge. Being in the centre of Mevagissey, you have walking access to some good pubs, cafés and the beautiful fishing harbour.

The interiors focus on comfort with licks of designer furniture, making it feel contemporary - we particularly like the chic designer lobby. Bedding is luxurious and the wet room has a rain shower and fluffy towels. It's bright and airy, but a cosy little hideaway that's perfect for exploring the meandering streets of this Cornish fishing harbour.

Maverick tip: If The Pilchard Press is fully booked, you should check out its equally stylish sister-propety Quay Loft.

quayside-meva.co.uk

The Pilchard Press, Photos by Bimble & Wander

Boutique Retreats

Photography by Matthew Heritage

From raising the flag on your own private island to watching the stars over the sea from your hot tub, Boutique Retreats specialise in unique properties that celebrate their surrounds whilst embracing luxurious living. That's why they're always our first port of call when planning a trip to the beautiful county of Cornwall.

With more than 140 luxury holiday rentals across Kernow, it's their passion to give guests a boutique hotel experience whilst providing privacy akin to their own homes. Large and luxurious or small but perfectly formed, their unique properties all share the same tip-top standard of luxury. Whether you're looking for a week in a seaside cottage, a chic waterside family home stay, a cliff top retreat with a private pool or a romantic weekend getaway in a countryside bolthole, their collection of retreats has been carefully hand-picked within the best areas of Cornwall.

Their team is on hand to help arrange those oh-so-special extras such as a private dining experience with a Michelin-starred chef, foraging with an expert, one-to-one surfing lessons or even something simple like a dog-sitter, you can be rest assured your Cornish escape will be one to remember. Over the next few pages, you'll find three of favourite properties from this unique bookings agency....

Trevail House

fowey

Trevail House is situated right on the water in the popular estuary town of Fowey. Set over three floors, expect gorgeous interiors, incredible facilities, plenty of space and a fabulous waterside terrace, plus it's dog friendly too. Inside, there's plenty of space to relax. The sitting room lies next to the kitchen on the first floor and has a host of original features such as the lovely fireplace. Next door you'll find the snug with its plush sofa, electric wood burning stove, fluffy bean bags and huge television with Apple TV and full Sky TV film and sports.

On the ground floor there's a handy study space for those who might need to catch up on some work, whilst the garden room is an informal space with fabulous kitchen facilities and a sofa for those who wish to sit inside and watch the world go by on the river. Fowey itself offers plenty to do, with a sandy beach, independent shops, top-notch restaurants and activities such as kayaking, sailing, boat hire or exploring the South West Coast Path.

From £2,063 for a long weekend or mid-week break, book at boutique-retreats.co.uk

Esperance Beach House

Whitsand bay

For those seeking a peaceful, chilled out coastal escape, look no further than this gorgeous seaside retreat. Tucked away on the cliffs in Whitsand Bay, Esperance is a stunning homestay for those seeking uninterrupted sea views in total luxury. The property is named after the town of Esperance in Western Australia, home to beautiful Cape Le Grand National Park which boasts the bluest, clearest waters imaginable. Step inside and you'll find stunning open-plan living that brings the outside in with floor-to-ceiling glass doors and blue views that give Cape Le Grand a run for its money.

Comfort is the name of the game, with sumptuous furnishings throughout and lots of little details to make your stay memorable. Outside, a bubbling hot tub and sun-drenched deck offers exceptional al fresco living, and it's dog friendly too. Should you be able to pull yourself away from this seaside escape, there's plenty to see and do nearby, whether it's sampling the finest seafood restaurants, hiking along coastal paths or exploring the picturesque villages that line the south coast.

From £1,172 for a long weekend or mid-week break, book at boutique-retreats.co.uk

Aphrodite Cottage

Tamar Valley

Step through the doors of this traditional Cornish cottage and you'll instantly fall in love with its characterful beauty, where whitewashed, endearingly wonky walls enclose a warm, welcoming haven for all who enter. The calming neutral tones, aged wooden beams and exquisite furnishings all lend themselves to creating a tranquil, calming space for both couples and families alike. Across the way is a hidden English country garden, where roses climb freely in the natural beauty of the secluded lawned area. There are sun beds to help top up your tan as well as patio area to enjoy a summer BBQ or just star gaze on a clear night.

Set close to Bodmin Moor next to a traditional working farm, this is perfect for those who love to explore on foot, whilst its ideal location means it's easy to reach both the North and South Cornish coasts. Also nearby is the beautiful Bodmin Moor and Tamar Valley or you can hop over the border to the market town of Tavistock and rugged Dartmoor.

From £721 for a long weekend or mid-week break, book at boutique-retreats.co.uk

Beaches & Coves

beautiful

TREBARWITH STRAND

Seemingly carved into the cliff, the descent down to Trebarwith Strand Beach is rocky and dramatic, opening up to a beautiful vista by the time you reach the bottom. It's worth checking the tide times, as this long stretch of beach can shrink significantly at high tide. At low tide it's a fabulous spot for rock-pooling and there are several caves worth exploring set within the cliffs. Locally, Trebarwith Strand is known as a surf beach, but it's suitable for intermediate and experienced surfers only.

PORTHCOTHAN BAY

You'll find family friendly Porthcothan Bay between Newquay and Padstow. It's a lovely, sizeable beach with beautiful rocky outcrops and clear waters. It's a bit of a hidden gem, but there are lots of campsites nearby, and in Porthcothan hamlet you can find a quaint village pub and a shop known for its excellent pasties.

CRANTOCK BEACH

Just a short drive from Newquay is dog friendly Crantock Beach. It's an expanse of soft golden sand, sheltered by a horizon of grassy dunes that provide a small workout when traversing or tumbling down them. There's also reliable surf at Crantock, where independent Big Green Surf School offer lessons and board hire.

PORTHCURNO

Beautiful, silky sand and stunning turquoise waters are the first things that come to mind when we picture Porthcurno Beach. It's not far from the similarly idyllic Pedn Vounder Beach (left) and it's a firm favourite among locals. Both beaches can get very busy around the peak summer season, so it pays to arrive early and grab a spot.

PERRANPORTH

This expansive beach on the north coast boasts miles of golden sands and great surf. It's easily accessible (making it ideal for families) and you'll find plenty of cafes and bars close by. There are also rock pools and sand dunes for children to explore, abundant with coastal wildlife.

KYNANCE COVE

Perhaps the most photographed destination in Cornwall, this tidal beach is located two miles north of Lizard Point and is famous for its white sands and turquoise waters. It's perfect for the adventurous, as low tide reveals its impressive rock stacks and hidden caves.

POLKERRIS BEACH

Polkerris is a safe and secluded Cornish cove, equipped with water sports hire, great for learning to windsurf, kayak or SUP. Facing southwest, the beach is ideal for catching glorious sunsets throughout the year and nearby Rashleigh Inn and Sam's on the Beach are both great spots for food.

TREGANTLE CLIFF BEACH

Tregantle Cliff Beach is part of Whitsand Bay in southeast Cornwall. It's a steep climb down to its lovely, unspoilt sand, so perhaps not the best choice for young children or the elderly. However, once you make it to the beach it's a great spot to catch the sunset. Dogs are welcome and there's a lifeguard on duty during summer.

Kynance Cove, Photo by Liam Alford

Kernow's

Independent
Shops

Cornwall is home to hundreds of brilliant
independent brick-and-mortar shops. In the age of
the Internet and the carbon copy chain store, these
local heroes are doing their bit to revitalise the high
street and provide discerning shoppers with a
special retail experience.

Alice in Scandiland, Photos by Rebecca Rees

ALICE IN SCANDILAND, LOSTWITHIEL

Alice Collyer knows a thing or two about curating a stylish home. After successfully launching her award-winning interiors blog back in 2017, she tested the retail waters by selling handpicked, vintage homewares from the She Shed in her garden. Fast forward a few years and the self-taught entrepreneur was opening the doors to her very own high street shop: Alice in Scandiland. Blending old and new is one of Alice's favourite tricks for creating a home with a story and soul. So naturally Alice in Scandiland is an homage to Contemporary Scandinavian/Nordic design and vintage homewares. A browse of this beautifully curated space will uncover everything from functional ceramics to playful art prints, handmade children's toys and unique mid-century furniture. Everything about the shop carries an air of playfulness, while remaining effortlessly stylish. So, if you're in the area make sure you drop by and say hello.

28 Fore Street, Lostwithiel

ST KEW FARM SHOP, BODMIN

If you're passing Bodmin on wheels and want to surprise your carful with an idyllic outdoor lunch, seemingly in the middle of nowhere, avoid the beaten track and make a stop at café and store St. Kew Farm Shop. We'd recommend browsing their fresh breakfast menu, full of the usual characters: avocado, sourdough, chipolatas, poached eggs and pancakes. They also serve Cornwall's finest Yallah coffee. Alternatively, you could head to their chicken shack on Friday evenings. There's outdoor seating amongst the apple trees for pints or a Pimms to go with their fried chicken or tempura vegetables. As their name suggests you can also pick up lots of colourful Cornish edibles from their abundant farm shop, or marvel at their small forest of houseplants. They also stock some unique home décor pieces like faux leopard skin rugs.

St Kew Highway, Bodmin

TRE, POL, PEN, TAMAR VALLEY

In case you don't speak Cornish 'Tre, Pol and Pen' means 'Home, Water and Earth' - three key elements to a well-fed life. Pretty fitting when you consider that this farm shop and restaurant in the Tamar Valley offers fresh Cornish ingredients, alongside local wines and spirits, and homewares from native makers. The shop is situated right at the entrance to Cornwall, near the Devon border, making it the perfect pit spot for holidaymakers looking to stock up on produce before driving deeper into the county. Open seven days a week, there's ample space for parking, a children's play area near to the restaurant, plenty of space for dogs to walk in the grounds and a large outdoor seating area. Tre Pol Pen also host regular events such as Pizza Fridays, murder mystery evenings and frequent workshops led by local artists and makers.

Lezant, Launceston

HORTUS DESIGN, MARAZION

You'll find our next shop, Hortus Design, in the historic market town of Marazion, overlooking the iconic St Michael's Mount. Owner Louis Hills is a houseplant aficionado and all-round design enthusiast. His impeccable taste has transformed the first floor of an old Georgian building into a tranquil, leafy oasis filled with a curated selection of homewares. You'll want to take your time exploring the shop, as there are plenty of jewels to be found amongst this indoor jungle.

We're all familiar with the benefits of filling our homes with greenery and let's face it, there's nothing better than the smug satisfaction of raising a happy, healthy houseplant. So, if you're unsure about how to style the plants in your own home, make sure you seek out Louis' expert advice during your visit.

West End, Marazion

WILLOW & STONE, FALMOUTH

Willow & Stone is a strong contender for our favourite independent shop in Cornwall. Purveyors of authentic ironmongery and unusual paraphernalia, you'll find their double fronted store on Falmouth's Arwenack Street and you won't miss their unique and creative window displays. This shop is a treasure-trove of beautiful things. Founder, Sarah Wilshaw, initially conceived of the business with the aim of providing quality, period ironmongery to ordinary people taking on extraordinary home restoration projects.

But the shop has evolved over the years into so much more. Today, Willow & Stone houses everything from colourful stationery to hand carved chopping boards, brass doorknobs, and cast-iron toilet roll holders. The shop itself is wonderfully styled and we could easily lose ourselves for a while browsing their vintage-inspired gift wraps and authentic period pieces. Just imagine you're renovating your dream home and let Willow & Stone do the rest...

8 Arwenack Street, Falmouth

unique pieces that you won't find just anywhere

BEAU SALA, WADEBRIDGE

Stacey Sibley is an interior designer with over 30 years' experience creating special spaces. Her brick-and-mortar shop and showroom in Wadebridge brings together this experience with unique pieces that you won't find just everywhere. Recognising that home decoration helps set apart a design scheme, Stacey selects a diverse range of sculptures, decorative ceramics and glassware.

Each accessory offers something a little different that breaks from the norm and is guaranteed to create an impression on your space. If you're visiting Cornwall on holiday and you want to recreate the magic of your trip at home, we recommend popping into the shop for some inspiration.

The Cedar Barns, Wadebridge

Onda, Photo by Goodrest Studios

ONDA, ST IVES

Arguably boasting the prettiest shop front
in all of St Ives, Onda is a brand-new
lifestyle store and rooms (see page 57) that
is sure to leave you feeling inspired. The
whole shop is a sort of visual mood-board
for beautiful living, offering freshly cut
flowers at the door along with a curated
selection of homewares, clothing, books
and toiletries.

17 Fore Street, St Ives

THE DUCHY OF CORNWALL NURSERY, LOSTWITHIEL

This next venue is so good it even gets the royal stamp of approval. This garden nursery houses hundreds of plants - both exotic and homegrown – as well as an award-winning café and a lifestyle shop. No matter what time of year you choose to visit, there's always something new to explore. Stroll through the bumblebee garden during summer or head to the café on a cold day and sit by the fire with a perfectly poured cup of coffee. Our favourite spot is the warm and inviting glasshouse (above) which is home to the most comprehensive range of indoor plants, cacti, succulents and air plants in the whole of the South West. The nursery is also a great spot to meet with friends for lunch. With views looking out to Restormel Castle you can relax with a glass of Camel Valley sparkling wine and enjoy a hearty lunch prepared with delicious local ingredients.

Cott Road, Lostwithiel

RECIPROCITY, SALTASH

Within the enchanting grounds of Port Eliot Estate, you'll find Reciprocity - a brand new, zero waste, lifestyle store and plant-based café that lives by the ethos of its namesake. Housed within the historic stable yard, visitors to the cafe can expect a menu of plant-based, seasonal and foraged foods, alongside locally sourced drinks and delicious coffee from Cornwall's very own Origin Coffee Roasters. Meanwhile, the shop itself is a calming space, filled with greenery and all manner of sustainable, eco-friendly wares.

Port Eliot Estate, Saltash

THE WEBB STREET COMPANY, FOWEY

The estuary town of Fowey is one of our favourite destinations in Cornwall. As well as boasting a myriad of brilliant eateries, it's filled with lovely independent shops. Take The Webb Street Company – this stylish lifestyle shop and gallery sits in the heart of the town and showcases simple, beautiful products designed to stand the test of time. Whether items are locally made or sourced from afar, everything from their elegant stationery to the handpicked artwork embodies living in Cornwall at its core.

2 Webb Street, Fowey

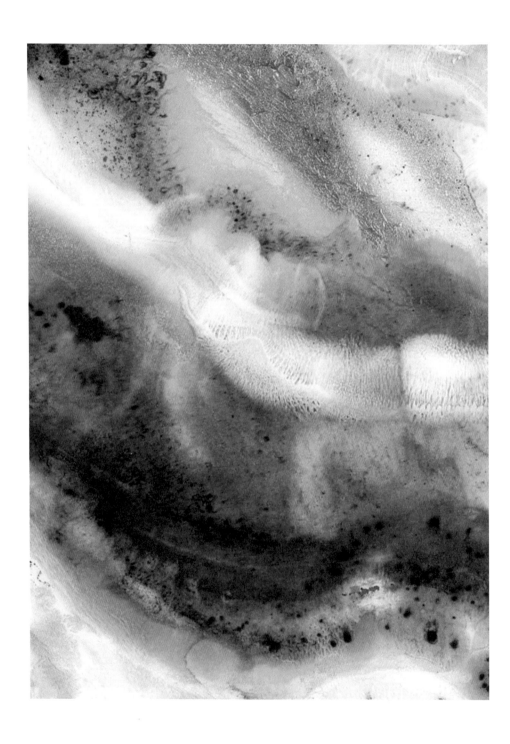

Maverick Meets

Zee van Gils

Zee van Gils' abstract seascapes are nothing short of mesmerising. Each glossy ripple of colour appears to have a mind of its own, fluid and unpredictable like the sea itself. The Dutch-born, Newquay-based artist has found a way to tell her own unconventional story through these unique resin artworks. Having traversed the globe in pursuit of her passions, Zee has spent the past decade mastering her medium of choice and embracing the transformative power of the ocean. Today, you'll be lucky to get your hands on one of her popular, abstract creations before they sell out. But it hasn't always been plain sailing for the 30-year-old artist and surfer...

By her own admission, Zee van Gils was an introverted child, who learned to express herself through her creativity. "Growing up in the Netherlands, I lived nowhere near the sea," she confesses. "It was a four-hour train journey to the coast, but I was always drawn to the ocean. I was always daydreaming, and I would pretend that the clouds were huge mountains. Everything in the Netherlands is completely flat, so creating these extreme landscapes was a sort of escape from reality."

At the age of 23, having side-tracked her creativity in favour of her academic studies, Zee felt the inexorable urge to discover the world beyond Dutch borders. Compelled to rekindle her childhood imagination, she packed her bags and swapped the flat landscape of canals and tulip fields for sandy beaches and warm waves. Little did she know that arriving on the island of Lombok, Indonesia, would trigger a cosmic chain of events.

"Lombok is where everything fell into place for me," says Zee. "It was the first place where I felt really good in myself, in both my body and my mind. I felt like I belonged there". Stripped of everyday luxuries, such as internet access and clean running water, Zee immersed herself in nature and through the act of simple living, found that all her creativity came flooding back.

As well as reigniting her imagination, Zee credits her move to Lombok for finding her calling in life. It was here where she truly connected with the ocean, learned to surf, and fell in love with her soulmate, Anthony (spoiler alert, he was her surf instructor).

"There's something almost spiritual about surfing," she explains. "It's helped me overcome quite a lot of mental health issues and physical insecurities. It pushes you both physically and mentally and it forces you to appreciate your body for what it can do, rather than criticising yourself for what you look like. I would say it has ruined my life in the best possible way. Since I first started surfing, everything has been about art, surf and being by the sea with my partner, just enjoying nature together."

When she wasn't in the ocean, Zee was busy balancing work as a surf photographer with her part time role at the local shaping bay. It was here, assisting the islands only surfboard shaper, where the final piece of the jigsaw fell into place. "I knew a guy who had broken his board in this crazy wave, and he ordered two new boards, which he asked me to paint. That was when I discovered resin. I was like: 'Oh my God, what is this?"

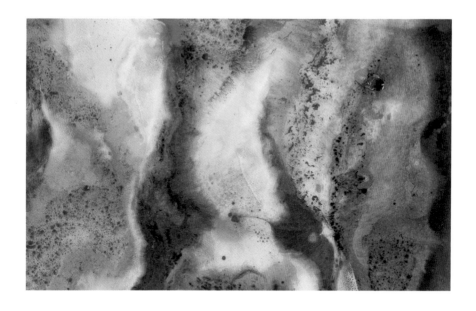

Resin is a vital component in the surfboard shaping process. The body of a board is made from fibreglass, and resin is used to harden the board's surface and to make it water resistant. Zee had never considered using it as an art material until she saw how puddles of resin would form when it dripped onto the floor. "All these textures were happening and the more I worked with the resin, I knew I was becoming completely obsessed. I started thinking about other ways I could use it to make art, and that's when the idea of the abstract paintings came in."

It's easy to lose yourself in one of Zee's resin paintings. There's an implication of movement – a dance of blues and iridescent pinks – as fluid and as unpredictable as the tides.

"I describe my work as abstract interpretations of the ocean from a merged perspective," she explains. "I try to capture the ocean simultaneously from an aerial view, but also from under the water's surface. I want to blend together textures, colours and the patterns to create one cohesive picture."

To achieve the desired result, Zee uses many different layers of resin to create a sense of depth. "During the process, I pour and heat the resin and then tilt it and I pop any air bubbles with a heat gun or a blowtorch. I have to wait for 12 hours between each layer and the clear topcoat has to dry for five days until I can hang it and ship it."

"I've always worked intuitively," she says. "I don't really use reference pictures because I have a lifetime of inspiration and visuals stored in my mind that I can draw from. Whenever I travel or go surfing, I feed this inspiration bank so I can keep pulling from it. When I start a painting, I usually just have the colours in mind and then I pour whatever feels right and work layer-by-layer. The composition and the textures tend to come together naturally. It's more reactive than planned. I only have partial control over the result because sometimes the materials can keep moving after I leave. I'll come back a couple hours later and the painting might look slightly different. That's what I love - I like the unexpected parts".

Of course, using an unconventional medium is not always plain sailing. As well as its unpredictable nature, working with resin requires a degree of trial and error. "I've been based in a few different climates now and they each present their own unique challenges," says Zee. "In Indonesia, the humidity affected how the resin moved and flowed. I was working from our bedroom in a bamboo house and the wood started warping in the heat and the resin took ages to set. I was also on a local wage – which was around £100 a month – and everything had to be imported from Australia, which was expensive. I couldn't even pay for health insurance at the time, yet I still invested in my art. I'm so lucky to have a studio here in Newquay where I can regulate the temperature!"

Zee's move to the surfing hub of Newquay was another seemingly random twist of fate. After happening upon a room for rent online, she and her partner decided to take the plunge. At the time, they were unsure where they would settle, as visa complications had seen them move from Lombok to Australia and back to the Netherlands in a constant state of flux. "Within two weeks of finding a room we had moved to Newquay," she laughs. "Our thought process was 'let's just take this opportunity and see where it goes!'"

"I feel super lucky to enjoy the lifestyle we have here in Cornwall. I mean, the weather is pretty shit, and the waves aren't always consistent, but you'll find friendly and positive vibes in the water." "Cornwall is peaceful and the people

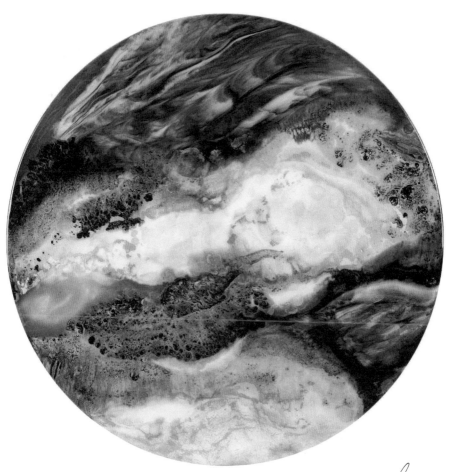

'Unbound' by Zee van Gils

tend to keep to themselves. I've noticed they apologise for things even when it wasn't their fault! Of course, there's a big difference between the surf here and in Lombok. In Indonesia you're surfing perfectly warm waves. Here, people are on a mission to get their surf in before it gets too cold, especially in winter."

Since making the move to Cornwall, Zee has taken the opportunity to focus on her art full time. It's a decision that has so far proved fruitful, with several commissions on the go and a myriad of collaborations under her belt. "I'm a pretty productive person," she says. "I usually have at least five to ten pieces on the go or in different stages".

Since landing in the county, Zee has collaborated with several Cornish makers, the likes of which include Hugh Brockman of BOS Surfboards in Penzance. But thanks to the power of social media, her art isn't just thriving within Cornwall's borders. "I also worked with Marion from Surfista Surfboards in Seignosse, France. She's one

of very few female board shapers and we got to know each other online. We always said we should work together but then Covid happened, and I couldn't get to France. One day I messaged her and said, 'let's just do this - I'll send you the artwork and you shape it!'. We both filmed our side of the process and together we created a colourful and unique board. It was cool to be able to collaborate from a distance."

With Cornwall as her base and an ocean of inspiration to draw from, it seems like Zee's creative journey is finally coming full circle. In 2019, she was lucky enough to realise one of her biggest career aspirations to date, when she got to collaborate with Californian brand, Album Surfboards. "They're a huge inspiration for me and Matt Parker is my favourite shaper. I always said, 'one day I'll work with him', so when that happened, I was like, 'OK, I'm done. I'm happy now!".

To discover more about Zee van Gils and to see what she's currently working on, visit her website at underthezee.com or give her a follow on Instagram: @underthezee

my Kernow

Frankie Thomas

Frankie Thomas is a freelance interior and food photographer based in central Cornwall. When she's not snapping photos of the county's hottest venues, you'll find her updating her popular Cornish lifestyle blog: 'Meet Me by the Sea'. We caught up with Frankie to find out her favourite things about life in Kernow...

How long have you lived in Cornwall?

I was born and grew up in Cornwall, however after completing my degree at Falmouth University, I decided to pack my bags and head to London for work. It only took a few years before I ached to be by the sea again. I adore the city, and part of me will always feel like London's home, but there's nothing quite like the Cornish lifestyle.

What makes Cornwall a great place to be based?

The Cornish lifestyle is extremely laid-back, which I've discovered is hard to find elsewhere. I put a lot of time and effort into my career, but I find that it's easier to differentiate work and play here in Cornwall, plus, there's nothing like a couple of hours at the beach to break up the working day!

Are there any downsides to living in such a remote place?

Like with everything there is a downside. Sometimes during the winter when the weather gets bad, it can feel quiet and hard to meet new people. I've also learnt that life in Cornwall is what you make of it and there are plenty of events, meet-ups and busy locations even during the quieter months — the hard bit is just finding them in the first place, but Instagram is definitely a saviour in that respect.

Where — in your opinion — is the most photogenic place to capture?

West Penwith (Lands End Peninsula) is by far my favourite part of Cornwall to photograph. The beaches from Zennor to Sennen and then around to Porthcurno are just magical. I genuinely believe that this area of coastline is home to some of the best beaches in the world. There are several secret beaches but they're best left to discover yourself. I also really love the National Trust spots in Cornwall — Trelissick is my favourite by far!

How do you relax during downtime?

I spend a lot of time looking after my wellbeing – being self-employed can be tough! Fortunately, we are blessed with miles of coastline and countryside to explore which instantly makes me feel better. I adore yoga and any activity that takes over the mind – that's probably why I always have a camera in my hand.

What do you do for fun?

I sell Cornish Prints via my Etsy shop (MeetMeByTheSeaStore) so I spend a lot of time running around Cornwall snapping away, creating prints. Other than that, I absolutely love my music so I'm always on the lookout for the next festival or Cornish gig. We are very lucky that our music culture is forever growing, especially post Covid. New events and festivals are popping up all the time – a few favourites include The Masked Ball, The Great Estate, Tunes in the Dunes and of course, Boardmasters.

Nanjizal Beach. Photo by Frankie Thomas

Pedn Vounder Beach. Photo by Frankie Thomas

Longstore Cocktails, Photo by Frankie Thomas

Longstore at Lemon Street is easily my favourite restaurant!

Frankie's Favourites

BEACHES FOR EXPLORING

Gwithian will always feel like home. My sister and I spent most of our childhood splashing around in the rockpools and bashing each other in the face with bodyboards in the waves. It really is a magical beach and I'm sure everyone that has visited will agree.

PLACE FOR DRINKS

Summer House in Perranporth is great for cocktails and the view across the beach is a real winner. As typical as it sounds, I also love going into Newquay for drinks – Cove24, Lewinnick Lodge and the Living Space at Watergate Bay Hotel are firm favourites.

COFFEE SHOPS

I love The Pantry at New Yard for coffee and light bites. You'll find it between the cobbled walls of the courtyard, a place where beauty lies in every direction, and wood fired pizza tastes like heaven.

RESTAURANT

The Longstore, Lemon Street is easily my favourite restaurant. The Longstore offers the finest steaks and seafood, locally sourced from the land and sea (you must try their Tomahawk Steaks). Expect a combination of city dining with a laid-back and welcoming atmosphere. They're also a photography client of mine, so I'm very lucky to be able to try some food on the job. I also recently visited Ugly Butterfly in Carbis Bay which was incredible.

CORNISH BRANDS

@thecovebathing – Cornish bath products.
@createdbyniki – Sea glass necklaces.
@santo_candle – Poured candles.
@no.1cubs – Clothing and coffee.

Find Frankie online at
meetmebythesea.co.uk
frankoethomas.com
@frankiethomas

Kernow's
Independent
Galleries

Since the 19th century, artists have been magnetically
drawn to the rugged and primal landscape of Cornwall.
Some say it's thanks to the light, others have credited
the slower lifestyle. So, it's no surprise that the county
harbours a huge community of creatives. But with
hundreds of noteworthy art galleries to choose from,
where does an art lover even begin? Thankfully, we've
chiselled the wide range of galleries down to a handful
of independent gems...

Morgans Gallery & Studios (previous page also Morgans)

MORGANS GALLERY & STUDIOS

Morgans is a relatively new addition to Cornwall's contemporary art scene, set over five storeys at the vibrant heart of Falmouth. This gallery and studio space was started by a family with years of combined industry experience, along with a deep-rooted passion for Cornwall. Owners Ann and Tony Morgan established the space with their three creative daughters – Martha, Ella and Clara – back in November 2019. Since they purchased the building, it has been extensively redesigned and renovated with the aid of local craftspeople and transformed into a truly beautiful and creative space. The gallery will play host to a rotation of exhibitions, showcasing work by young and emerging talent, alongside well-established names. Meanwhile, the three storeys above the gallery are dedicated studio spaces for practising artists.

You can expect a break from tradition with the work showcased at Morgans. A typical exhibition blends together painters, ceramicists and makers, with a particular emphasis on work by young female artists, the likes of which include rising stars Julia Florence and Martha Homes.

CORNWALL CONTEMPORARY

Walk to the top of Chapel Street in Penzance and you'll find Cornwall Contemporary. This much-loved gallery recently celebrated its fifteenth anniversary, with gallery director Sarah Brittain-Mansbridge at the helm, and in that time, it has developed a reputation for showcasing high quality, unique works and for spotting regional talent. Wander to the top of its three floors for marvellous rooftop views of Penzance. For sale, you'll find a mix of established British artists beside promising just-out-of-art-school finds. The gallery mainly emphasise art that has a connection to the region – not just paintings, but ceramics, jewellery, and sculpture too. Recently they showcased David Mankin's popular works; emotive and abstract paintings of the Cornish landscape (Sennen, Mousehole). Their winter collection is due to be showcased from 10 November 2021 – 21 February 2022.

Cornwall Contemporary, 'Encounters' exhibition by David Mankin.

Anima Mundi Gallery, 'Concerning The Fragile' exhibition by Andrew Litten

ANIMA MUNDI, ST IVES

Going against the grain of London-centric art galleries, this excellent space in St. Ives embraces the slower pace of Cornwall and the region's ability to bring us closer to our natural surroundings. Not a typical Cornish gallery, Anima Mundi exhibits a thrilling collection of contemporary work from around the globe. Each of its innovative artists are not so much linked by style, but in their ability to be thought provoking. Set in a quiet side street, in a former Christian Science reading room, Anima Mundi stretches over three light-filled floors. Past exhibitions have showcased works by esteemed artists such as Rebecca Harper, Andrew Litten and Carlos Zapata.

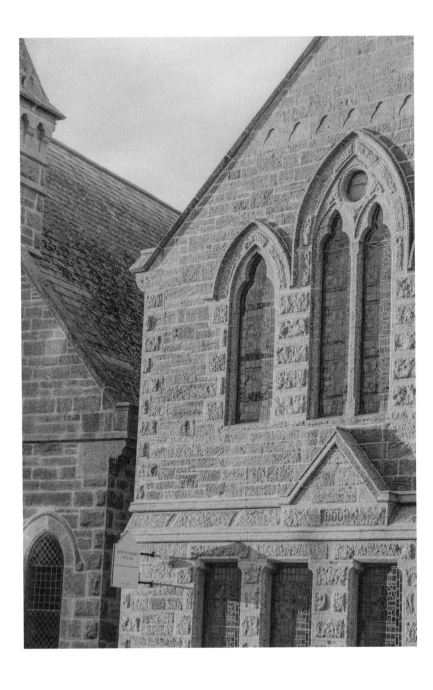

NORTH COAST ASYLUM

Set in a lofty gothic church hall not far from Towan Beach, North Coast Asylum is a seriously exciting artistic venture. This beautifully lit space is bright and airy and radiates with the sunlight that pours in through its original stained-glass windows. The gallery and event space was masterminded by Jo and Ben, a duo of seasoned art professionals with previous experience at Christie's auction house. Now based in Newquay, they aim to nurture a community of artists and provide a place to exhibit their work. The surrounding ocean and coastline features in much of the artwork on show and, although coastal-inspired work is frequently seen in Cornwall, their collection is genuinely innovative, born out of promising emerging talent. We suggest taking an afternoon out to stroll around this creative space and absorb the calming influence of the work on show.

LIVINGSTONE ST. IVES

St. Ives has long been associated with its thriving artistic community, thanks largely to the unique quality of its light. So, when Livingstone gallery was founded in 2020, it continued to build on the town's artistic legacy. The space itself is a welcoming and almost homely space — two converted fishing cottages now decked out with rugs and furniture for visitors. So, you can spend an afternoon looking over bold oil paintings that are bursting with colour and eye-popping ceramics from the comfort of a sofa. Walls feature exciting 21st century artists such as Emily Powell, Isobel Litten and Layla Andrews. If you fall in love with any of their pieces, Livingstone also offers a unique try before you buy service!

my Kernow

Jenifer Rosena

Jenifer Rosena is a twenty-something, born and bred on a beef farm on Bodmin moor. She shares her explorations around the county across her beautifully curated social media accounts. For the foodies, she shares all the best independent Cornish eateries on @eatdrinkcornwall, her daily life is documented at @jeniferrosena and she demonstrates that Cornwall is more than just a beautiful coastline over at @cornersofcornwall.

How long have you lived in Cornwall?

Apart from moving away to university in Bournemouth for a few years, I've always lived in Cornwall and probably always will!

What makes it a great place to be based?

For me, Cornwall offers such a variety of life and endless inspiration. One day I want to feel small strolling on Bodmin Moor, the next I'm living the coastal dream with sea swims and sunsets but if I fancy immersing myself in history, enjoy cocktails in town or spending my day in a gallery - Cornwall can offer all of that too and all within a very short drive from home.

Are there any downsides to living in such a remote place?

When I was younger, I certainly thought so! Being a teenager, before I could drive, it was difficult to do what I felt other kids my age were doing. However, as I have gotten older, I find joy in all those things I once struggled with.

Where - in your opinion - is the most photogenic place to capture?

The hardest question to answer, so many to choose from! I absolutely love Porthgwarra, I find something so magical about that place. The walk from Porthgwarra to Nanjizal is a photographer's dream. Some of my favourite photographs are also from a visit to Helford Village, the thatched cottages are so incredibly beautiful.

What do you do for fun?

Despite living in Cornwall all my life, there's still so many places left for me to explore, so I like to get out as often as possible and head to a new cove, village or part of the coastline. My perfect day out includes beautiful scenery, getting my feet wet in the sea and a delicious lunch.

How do you relax during downtime?

Whenever it's bad weather, I love crafting and making things - my latest favourite is making anything and everything out of air-drying clay. During lockdown, with the roads so quiet, I took up skateboarding. When it's lovely outside, you'll often find me on the moors skating along the road as the sun is going down.

Polruan Village, Photo by Jenifer Rosena

St Ives

the thatched cottages are incredibly beautiful

Helford Village

Jenifer's Favourites

BEACH FOR EXPLORING

Everyone in Cornwall has a favourite beach - usually one from their childhood - and mine is Daymer Bay. One I have so many memories on, building sandcastles as children, trying to get our first puppy to enjoy swimming in the sea and endless picnics and nights watching the sunset from the cliff top.

PLACE FOR DRINKS

The rooftop bar at Salt Box in Wadebridge has been lovely this summer, they have a pizza place and other takeaway food downstairs too so it's the perfect evening.

RESTAURANT

With running my Eat Drink Cornwall account, it encourages me to constantly try new places, which I love. One of my all-time favourites has to be Strong Adolfos on the Atlantic Highway, they do incredible breakfast and lunch. For an evening meal, the best food I've eaten recently was at Temple in Bude. An incredible three course meal made with the freshest, local ingredients.

COFFEE SHOP

I've recently become obsessed with chai latte and I must say one of the best ones I've had so far was from Lands End Container - a little converted shipping container near Sennen.

CORNISH BRANDS & CREATORS

Oh, so many! I love the Coconut Bee natural skincare products and no kitchen is complete without Cornish Seasalt. I adore Katy Pillinger who produces beautiful artwork, I buy all my cards from her and Nina Brooke for the most calming seascapes.

There are so many beautiful Cornish content creators out there! Some of my favourites are: @georgiescorner, @travelandthegirls @frankiethomas, @seaview_gunwalloe

Find Jenifer online at
jeniferrosena.com
@cornersofcornwall

ultimate Bucket List

With so much to see and do during your visit to Cornwall, it can be hard to know where to start. Luckily for you, we've compiled a hit-list of the county's must-see attractions and unique experiences...

HIT THE WAVES

If there's one thing Cornwall is famous for – outside of the humble pasty – it's gorgeous beaches and great surf. So, if you fancy getting to grips with a surfboard there are few better places to learn. **Freewave Surf Academy** is a surf school with over fifteen years' experience in taking small groups, families and individuals on surfing lessons and aquatic adventures in and around Widemouth Bay in Bude. Their team of local instructors will get you riding the waves in no time!

Of course, if you're already an accomplished surfer, you'll probably want to hit the county's best surf spots: Fistral Beach, Watergate Bay, Godrevy Beach, Porthtowan or Constantine Bay.

CONNECT WITH THE OUTDOORS

If it's nature you seek, there are plenty of outdoor activities and wild camping sites to scratch that itch. As well as teaching a variety of surfing classes, **Wave Cornwall** let you sleep under the stars at their hand-crafted woodland campsite. This purpose-built wild camp is perfect for groups, as it's hidden away in the heart of the Cornish countryside. If you like the sound of an action-packed weekend, filled with wild swimming trips, axe throwing and sharing stories around a campfire, then make sure you check out their Adventure Weekend Getaways. Alternatively, just embrace the serenity of the surrounding woodland with some restorative yoga and fire up the BBQ for an al fresco feast.

For a campsite with a difference, look no further than **Kudhva**. These guys take off-grid accommodation to the next level with their unique architectural cabins, specifically designed for the quarry-rich environment they inhabit. These hideouts look a little bit like they've been plucked from a science fiction novel, raised high above the ground, standing on wooden legs with a suspended bed and captivating views down the coast. You could also opt to stay in their authentic Danish Cabin; with trees growing through its deck and a babbling stream winding underneath its stilt frame.

If rural relaxation is on the cards, head to **Botelet**. Hidden up-stream from Fowey, this special venue has been farmed, nurtured and styled by the Tamblyn family for 150 years. It's an idyllic retreat that lets you slip away from the hustle and bustle of everyday life to embrace a sense of tranquillity and calm. Choose to stay in one of three historic self-catering cottages or sleep close to nature in a yurt, positioned in its own peaceful orchard.

With therapeutic massage, retreats, meditation classes, creative and wellbeing courses taking place throughout the year, there's always a good reason to make a trip to Botelet.

ENJOY A ONE-OF-A-KIND PICNIC

Pretty as a Picnic is a bohemian picnic set-up service that's all about displaying quality produce beautifully. Their pop-up picnics can be ready and waiting for you and your party at a location of your choice, complete with everything you could possibly need for a memorable event. Expect fabulously decorated tables filled with sharing boards that are piled high with cheese, fruit, charcuterie and nibbles of every variety. They'll even bring the glassware, fresh flowers and decorative touches like candles, fairy lights and rose petals. The best part? They do the washing up too!

181

IMMERSE YOURSELF IN MYTH AND LEGEND AT TINTAGEL CASTLE

Kernow is a land steeped in myth and legend and nowhere can this be felt more strongly than at Tintagel Castle. Set high on Cornwall's rugged north coast, these atmospheric ruins are inextricably linked with the legends of King Arthur. Once a stronghold for early medieval rulers, Geoffrey of Monmouth named Tintagel as the place where King Arthur was conceived. It seems likely that such legends inspired Richard, Earl of Cornwall, to build his impressive cliff-top castle on the site in 1233.

Today, thanks to English Heritage, you can take in the stunning natural scenery and explore these 13th century ruins. Imagine feasting in the heart of Lord Cornwall's court and follow in the footsteps of Cornwall's medieval inhabitants as you cross the footbridge to the island with waves crashing beneath you. Outdoor displays guide you through the history of the castle and the role that legend has played in shaping the historic site. You don't want to miss out on a photo op with the brooding Gallos, either. He's a life-sized bronze sculpture inspired by the legend of Arthur and he's all too happy to star in your selfies!

Tintagel Castle from above, Photos © English Heritage

turn soft and pliable clay into wonderful pots

LEARN TO THROW POTTERY

Home to the iconic striped Cornish ware and the world-famous Leach Pottery – we guarantee you'll want to get your hands on your own ceramic memento during your trip to Kernow. The county isn't short of places to learn to throw pottery either. Fans of The Great Pottery Throwdown will no doubt recognise Sally Tully, who repped Cornwall with her brilliant creations in the 2021 season of the Channel 4 show. Now Sal shares her talents through pottery workshops at her studio, **Sally Tully Ceramics** in St Keverne, near Helston. Aspiring potters can book a class to learn how to turn soft and pliable clay into wonderful pots. You'll look at various methods of making and decoration techniques and you'll leave with your own fabulous creation!

SINK A PINT AT THE JAMAICA INN

As well as being the namesake of a much-loved Daphne Du Maurier novel, this ancient inn was made famous as a drinking spot for smugglers and wreckers in days gone by. Today, it's a living piece of history and a working pub, serving up tasty food surrounded by the wild and beautiful landscape of Bodmin Moor.

ENCOUNTER BLUE SHARKS

Feeling brave? Dive into the ocean depths and get up close and personal to blue sharks with **Newquay Sea Safaris**. But don't start humming the Jaws theme just yet - blue sharks are beautiful and highly inquisitive creatures. You'll be able to spy these sleek predators from the safety of an underwater cage, and you'll leave with newfound knowledge about the plight of British sharks and how to support their conservation.

THE SOUTH WEST COAST PATH

Cornwall's coastline boasts the UK's longest and best-loved National Trail: The South West Coast Path. With 19th century origins (as a coastguard patrol route to restrict smuggling), today the Coast Path is England's longest way-marked footpath. It runs for 630 miles, from Minehead on the edge of Exmoor to the shores of Poole Harbour, stretching along the vast majority of Cornwall's coast.

Start your journey in North Cornwall, where the land is alive with flora and fauna. Highlights include: the iconic twin-headland of The Rumps; the stunning wildflowers of West Pentire; the foodie haven of Padstow and the beaches of Polzeath; Harlyn Bay; Watergate Bay and Newquay.

Heading west will lead you along scenic sandy beaches like Holywell Bay and Perranporth, before arriving in artsy St Ives. Discover the iconic Mount's Bay, site of the magical St Michael's Mount, and stroll through the picturesque coastal village of Mousehole. You'll also have the chance to stand on the southernmost tip of England at The Lizard peninsula.

Southern Cornwall offers the most sheltered stretch of The South West Coast Path with impressive headlands and some of the prettiest towns in the county. After crossing the Fal Estuary you'll arrive on the Roseland Peninsula. Along the way you'll pass the charming harbour towns of Charlestown and Mevagissey, as well as the estuary town of Fowey and its sister village Polruan. Later, the great sweep of Whitsand Bay will take you to Cornwall's 'forgotten corner': The Rame Peninsula. Here you'll be treated to tidal creeks, sandy beaches, rolling fields and outstanding country parks.

Find out more information online at southwestcoastpath.org.uk

FALL UNDER THE SPELL OF THE MUSEUM OF WITCHCRAFT & MAGIC

The picturesque village of Boscastle on the North Cornwall coast is home to one of the UK's most beloved and unusual attractions: **The Museum of Witchcraft & Magic.** Set over two floors, the museum has 25 permanent displays and over 7000 objects and curiosities to discover. There's everything from magical tools - such as glass knitting needles, black mirrors, and crystal balls - to unique artefacts such as protection talismans made by soldiers in the trenches of World War One. The concept behind the museum is to represent the diversity of magical practices through a respectful and impartial lens.

DISCOVER THE CAMEL TRAIL

If you can tear yourself away from the coast, Cornwall offers an abundance of green countryside to explore. The best way to take advantage of this scenery is by walking or cycling the **Camel Trail.** Following a disused railway line, this scenic trail follows the Camel Estuary from Padstow to Wadebridge before heading through the beautifully wooded Camel Valley to Bodmin. The whole 18-mile trek is more or less traffic free, making it an ideal day out for the whole family. No bike? Don't worry, you can hire them from several venues in Padstow, Wadebridge or Bodmin, or simply take in the scenery by foot.

SLEEP IN AN OLD JAIL CELL

While at first this experience might not sound too appealing, the beautifully renovated **Bodmin Jail Hotel** offers a range of luxurious suites to lay your head down. Sensitively restored and painstakingly preserved, the hotel is the showpiece of a £50 million renovation project which has seen the walls of an 18th century prison transformed into a 4-star boutique hotel. Behind original cell doors you'll find free-standing baths, walk-in showers and indulgent bedding – all set against the backdrop of weathered stone walls. The striking glass ceiling of the hallway bathes the corridors with sunlight and provides beautiful sky views. And, with three onsite eateries to choose from, guests can indulge in afternoon tea, hand-made pastries or something extra special, with tempting menus paying homage to locally sourced ingredients from Cornwall's finest food producers.

THE LOST GARDENS OF HELIGAN

Sister attraction to the famous Eden Project, The Lost Gardens of Heligan houses over 200 acres of tropical and native plants. It's an epic restoration project that saw an expansive Victorian estate revitalised into a sub-tropical oasis. With towering palms, feathery ferns and leafy giant rhubarb, Heligan is good for both couples who want to get lost in its wild, romantic gardens, and families looking to ignite their imagination.

MEET FRIENDLY GREY SEALS

There's a reason seals are often called the dogs of the sea. Not only are they adorable, but they're playful and intelligent creatures. Grey seals are native to our coastlines and can be spotted in the wild throughout Cornwall. To guarantee a sighting, visit **The Cornish Seal Sanctuary**; a charity that rescues and rehabilitates grey seal pups from around Cornwall. Several underwater viewing areas let you get up close to these lovely animals and children can get involved through interactive feeding sessions and daily educational chats.

UNWIND AT A LUXURY CORNISH SPA

For head-to-toe relaxation, there are few
better places than The Scarlet Hotel. Their
eco spa features a bromine-filtered indoor
pool, an outdoor natural reed pool and a
restorative steam room. Treatments take
place in tented, lantern-lit rooms and
include a stillness session after in the deep
relaxation room's suspended cocoon pods.
For a true bucket-list worthy experience,
plunge into the clifftop hot tub and look out
over the blue Atlantic.

WATCH A PERFORMANCE AT THE EXTRAORDINARY MINACK THEATRE

The word Minack translates to 'rocky place' in
the Cornish tongue, which is pretty apt when it
comes to describing this unique, open-air
theatre. Carved out of the steep granite cliffs
overlooking Porthcurno Bay, The Minack Theatre
is a real modern marvel of construction, largely
built by the hands of one woman: Rowena Cade.
Audiences of the theatre are treated to
panoramic views out across the sea, as well as
an exciting line-up of live musical and theatrical
performances, that run from May to September
each year.

Notes